Minhwa
Workbook

Minhwa
Workbook

Step-by-Step Guide to Korean Folk Painting

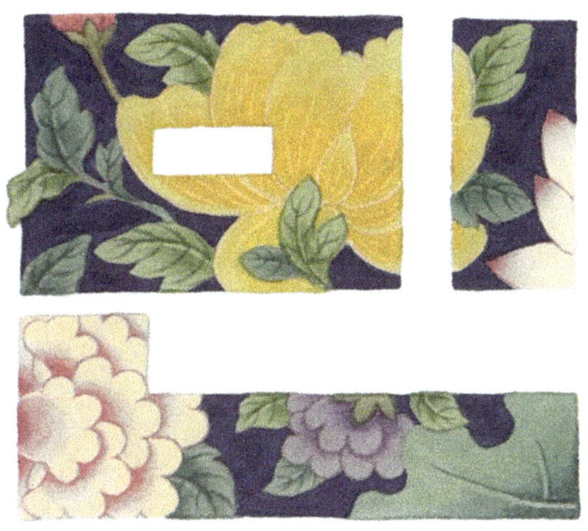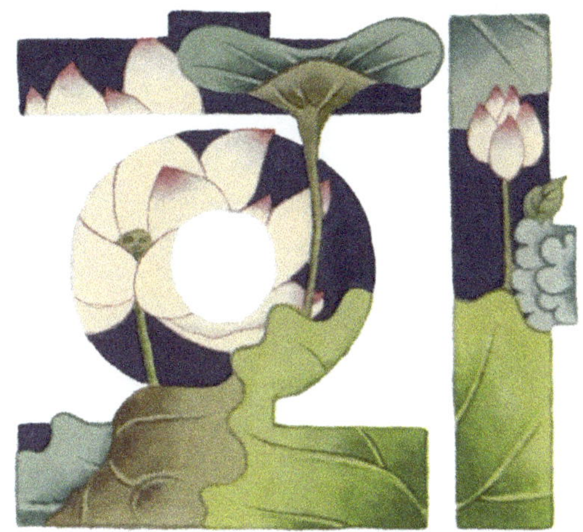

Hye-Ryung Suk

Translated & Edited by
Seo Choi

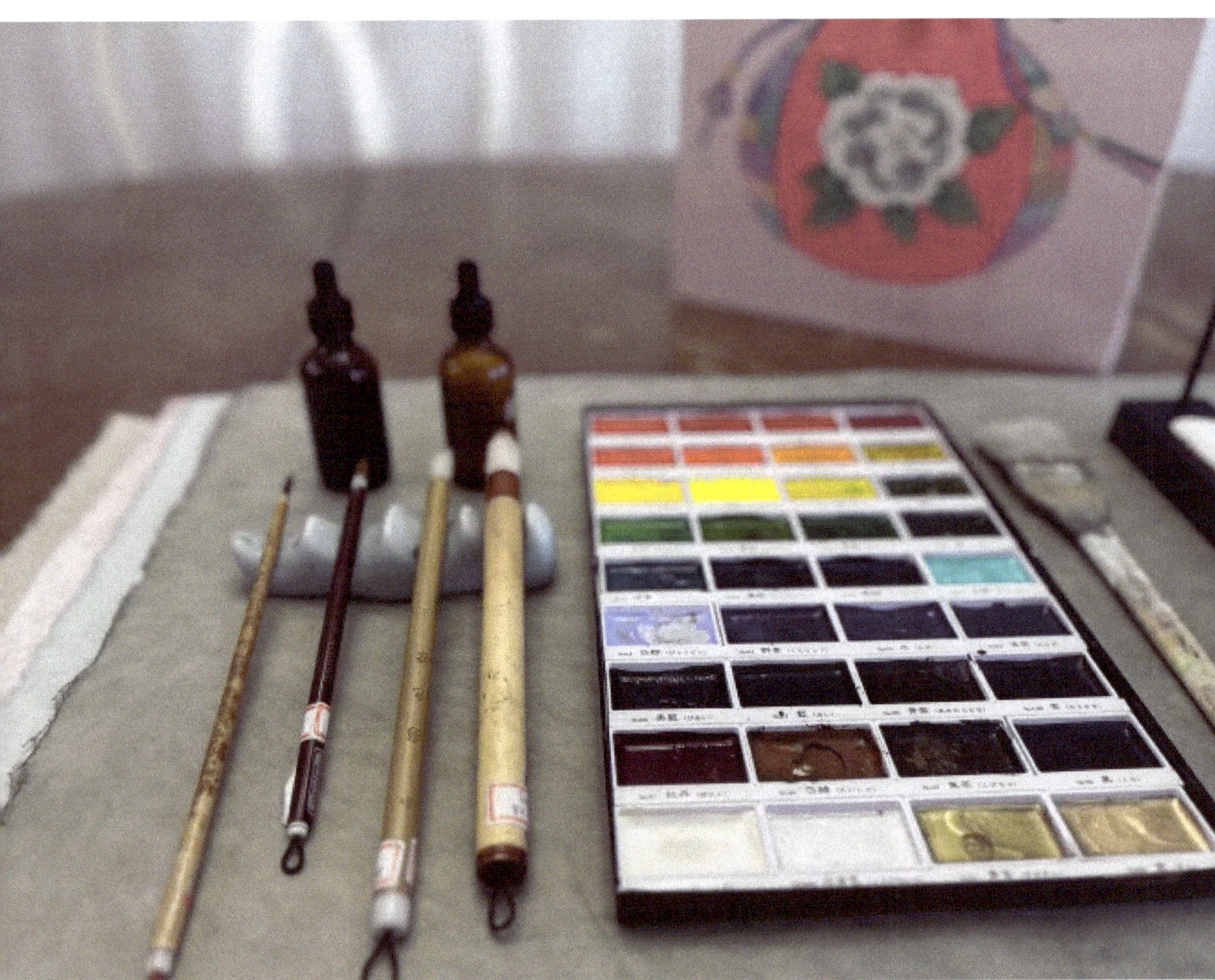

Table of Contents

Publisher's Note   vii

Introduction   viii

Minhwa Paintings Step-by-Step   1

   Minhwa Tools

   Making a Minhwa Canvas

   Paper Preparation

   Outlining the Design

   Mounting the Outlined Artwork

   Coloring — Mindful Layers

   Finishing Touch

Making Minhwa Today   37

Practice Arts   46

   Popular Minhwa Symbolism

   Practice Arts (Color & Outline)

Resources   95

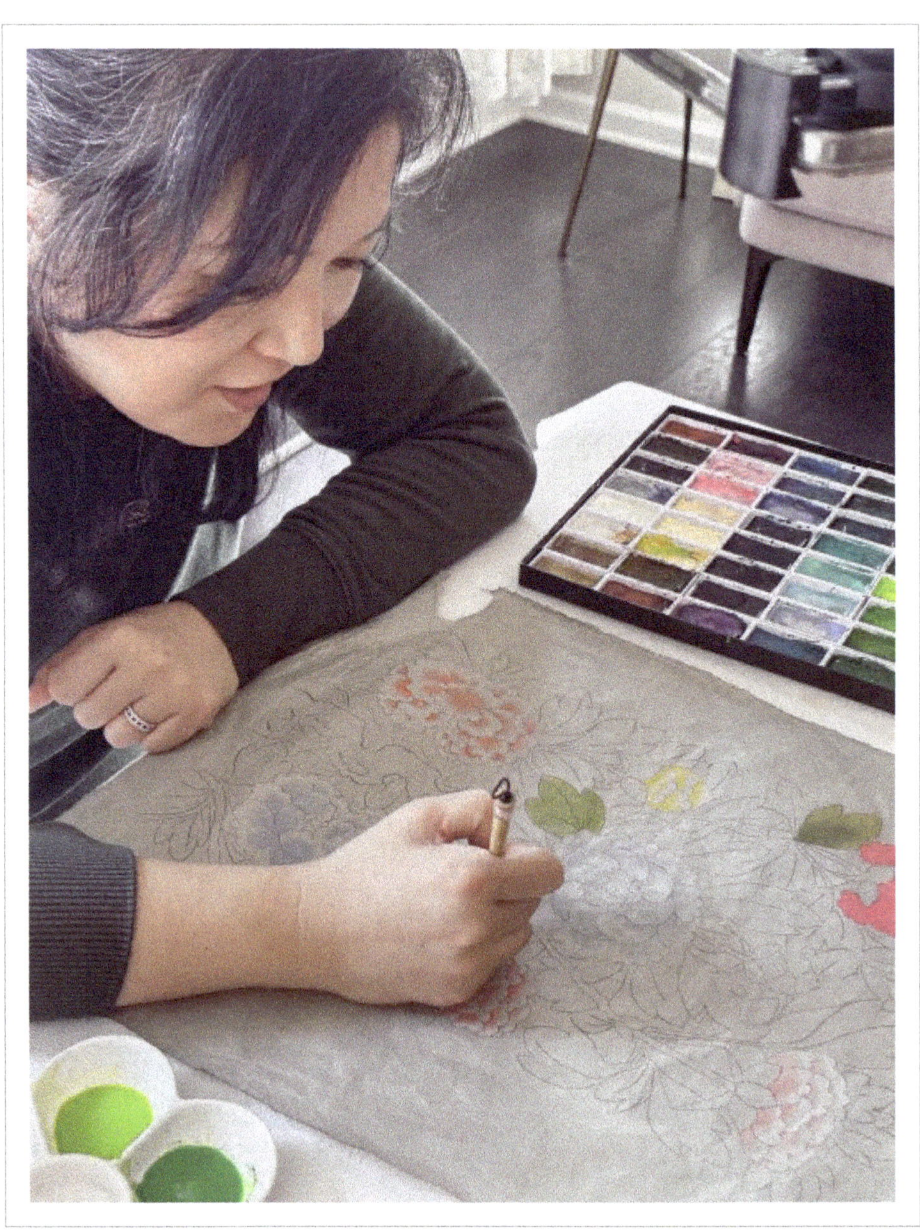

Our Ancestral Art as Medicine

Min (the people) + Hwa (painting)

Here, min does not translate as any people or all people. It refers to the Korean word baekseong, which means people who are ruled. The "folk" of "folk art."

Minhwa (민화) is a genre of Korean folk art that originated during the ancient Joseon dynasty (1392–1897 CE). This period was characterized by a Confucian society where the noble class, known as the yangban, held all the power and privileges. It was a patriarchal society in which women across all social classes were largely disempowered and had very few rights. However, in the later years of the Joseon period, people outside the dominant ruling class *began* to explore their artistic expressions, leading to a significant rise in folk art.

The late Joseon period created many popular art forms, including fictional tales and pansori music. Mask dance plays, acrobatic dancing, and various performances entertained the populace by satirizing their everyday lives.

Minhwa provides unique insight into the arts outside the dominant narrative—art forms created by our ancestors who faced injustice, inequality, and restrictions on their freedom. For some readers, studying minhwa can be a form of ancestral healing.

The spiritual aspect of minhwa is something I only became aware of while working on this book. Minhwa also acted as a talisman, embodying people's hopes, wishes, and prayers. By mindfully and intentionally preparing the paper, selecting colors, and crafting the art, they painted minhwa to invite blessings for their families and loved ones. If this isn't an example of healing art, I don't know what is.

We were thrilled to share extensive information about minhwa, but we also aimed to create a user-friendly guide that anyone can utilize in their creative practice.

With this book, may you receive the joy and healing of ancestral art as medicine.

Seo Choi
Publisher

My Story with Minhwa

I remember when I first began learning about minhwa. I had just graduated with a degree in Western Fine Arts, which was quite competitive then. I attended my first minhwa class with a sense of superiority, believing that the folk art of my ancestors would be primitive and simple. However, I was quickly humbled as I started to learn the intricacies of the art.

As I studied and practiced minhwa, I became increasingly amazed by our ancestors' aesthetic style, creativity, unrestricted composition, vivid colors, and humor. Initially, I had believed that minhwa lacked the artistic value of Western Fine Arts, such as oil painting. That misconception was utterly shattered, and I felt ashamed of my previous prejudice. I also experienced immense pride in knowing I carry the same DNA as these incredible artists. In their work, I discovered beauty and wisdom that are as powerful and inspiring as the masterpieces of beloved artists like Monet, Cezanne, and Van Gogh.

What surprised me most about minhwa was its beauty and its intricate creation process. Completing a single piece of art requires significant care and effort, especially in the preparation stage. This meticulous process begins with hanji, a traditional Korean paper made using a unique technique.

A special solution is carefully mixed with a precise combination of agyo glue and alum. After being applied to the paper, it is air-dried and then prepared with a natural dye to create the base for minhwa. The preparation involves considering the day's temperature and humidity, ensuring smooth and even brushstrokes, and multiple rounds of air-drying, either by hanging the paper on strings or laying it flat on the floor.

This tedious and time-consuming process demands a great deal of patience. Just as iron is forged in fire and turned into a strong weapon, this lengthy preparation transforms the thin and delicate hanji paper into a sturdy foundation capable of withstanding multiple layers of brushstrokes and colors.

Learning about this art form made me recognize the connection between the resilience of the Korean people, who have thrived and survived through many years of foreign invasions and trauma, and the effort that goes into creating minhwa.

Minhwa, which translates to "people's painting," is not created by professionally trained artists. Instead, it refers to folk paintings made by everyday people during the Joseon dynasty. These paintings depict subjects from daily life, including flowers, insects, animals, birds, rocks, and trees.

What is particularly interesting is that these different subjects carry specific meanings and intentions. People painted them to wish for luck and blessings. For example, a fish transforming into a rising dragon symbolizes hope for children's success, while peonies represent wealth and fortune. Peaches and butterflies signify the desire for parents' long lives and health, and flowers and birds symbolize love and respect among family members.

Minhwa is a form of art created with well-wishes and love for others. It transforms metaphysical dreams and desires into tangible artwork. Minhwa is a unique cultural artifact of our ancestors and a testament to their values and hopes.

When I immigrated to the U.S. a few years ago, my new home country felt immense and overwhelming. The vastness of the land sometimes made it feel barren and lonely. Living as a "foreigner" in a country built on land soaked with the blood of indigenous peoples left me feeling afraid and unfamiliar. Despite

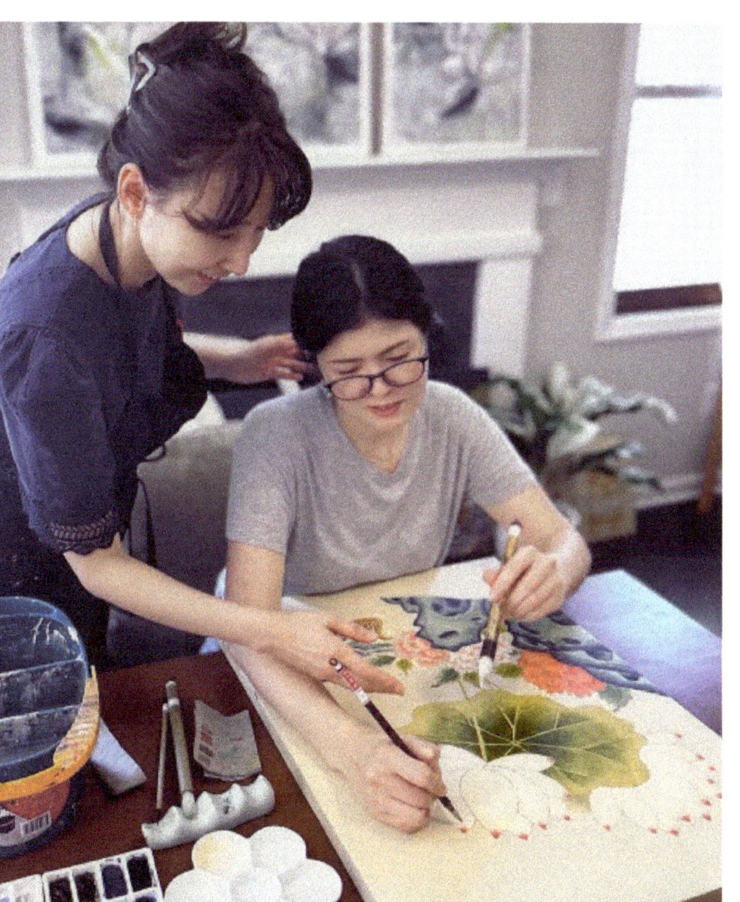

being an adult, I felt as though I had to relearn everything from the language to the rules of the road. During that time, I often experienced terrible homesickness, missing my family and friends in Korea. However, minhwa became a familiar companion for me.

As I painted, I expressed my longing and loneliness through vibrant layers of color. Those layers of sadness transformed into butterflies, dragons, and flowers, flying away into the world. Gradually, people who were interested in minhwa began to find me. This art form brought me valuable new friendships and connections in my new country. Like a swallow bringing good news, I unexpectedly received the opportunity to share the wisdom and beauty of minhwa with a broader audience through a book. What a magical gift minhwa has been! I am deeply inspired and grateful for this wonderful gift of dreams coming true, brought to life through these paintings.

I hope everyone who reads this book feels inspired to dream and create beauty in their lives just as our ancestors did. They endured hardships by transforming their struggles into blessings and dreams through art. Whether these dreams come to fruition or not, a life enriched by art, dreams, and resilience is truly worth living. I firmly believe that when people aspire to experience beauty and love, even in challenging times, the universe gradually brings those dreams to life. Minhwa can serve as a companion, guiding you toward a life filled with happiness and resilience.

Hye-Ryung Suk
Author
IG @atlanta_minhwa

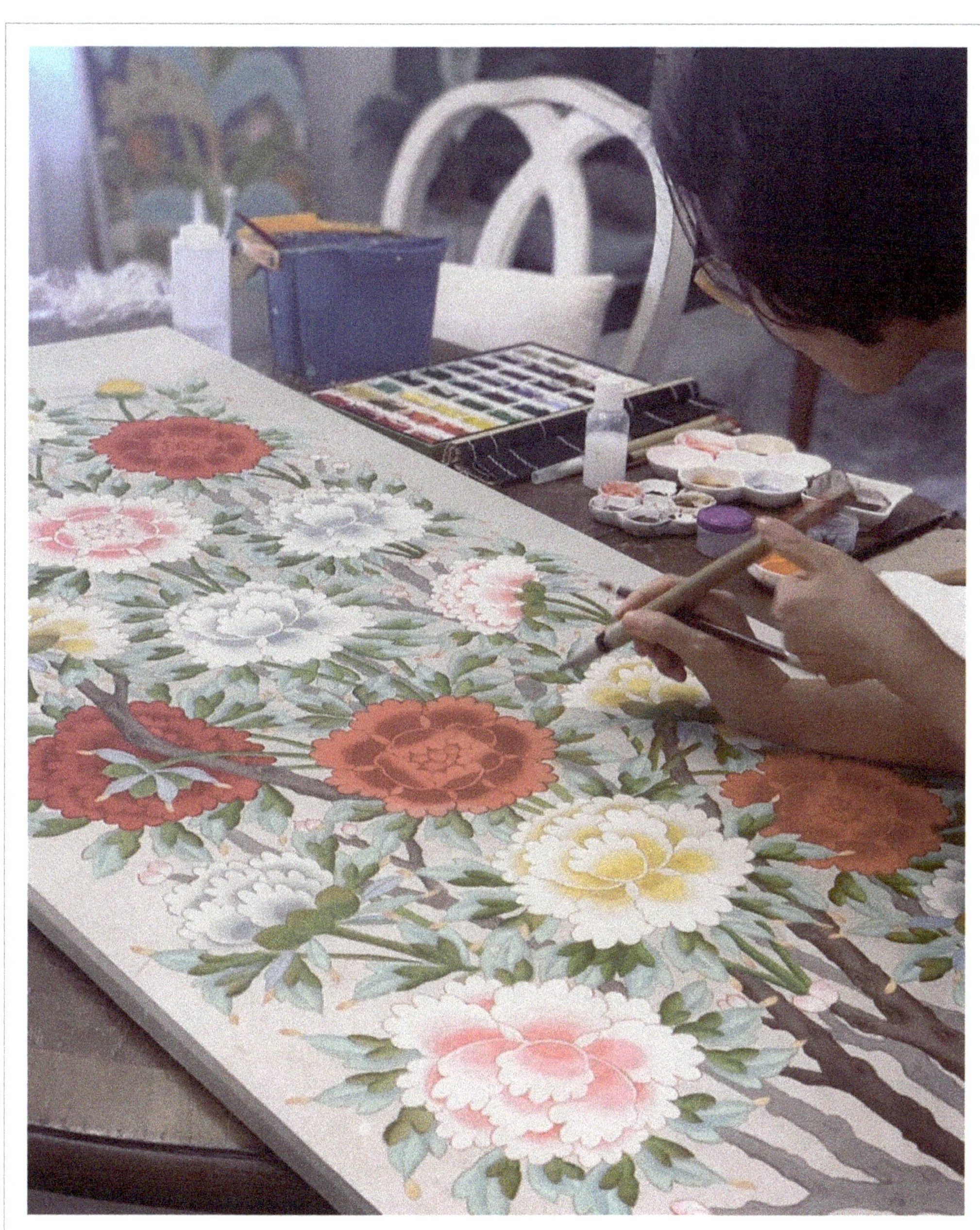

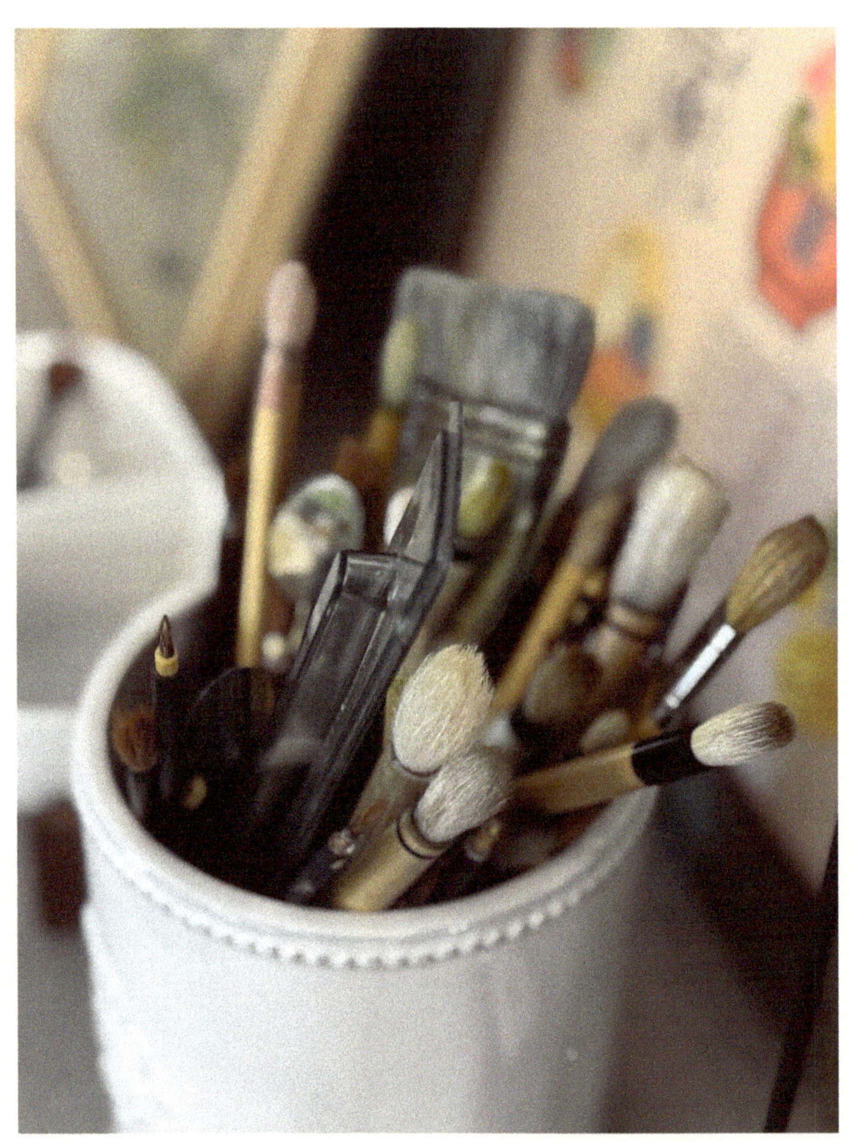

Minhwa Paintings Step-by-Step

❀ Minhwa Tools ❀

Minhwa is a genre of Eastern Fine Arts (dongyanghwa), encompassing paintings primarily from China, Japan, and Korea. Artists in this tradition use specialized tools designed for these types of paintings. While papers, pigments, brushes, and other necessary materials can be found at many fine art shops in Asia, they may be more difficult to acquire in the West. However, several retailers offer international shipping; please refer to the Resources section of this book for more information.

Hanji Paper

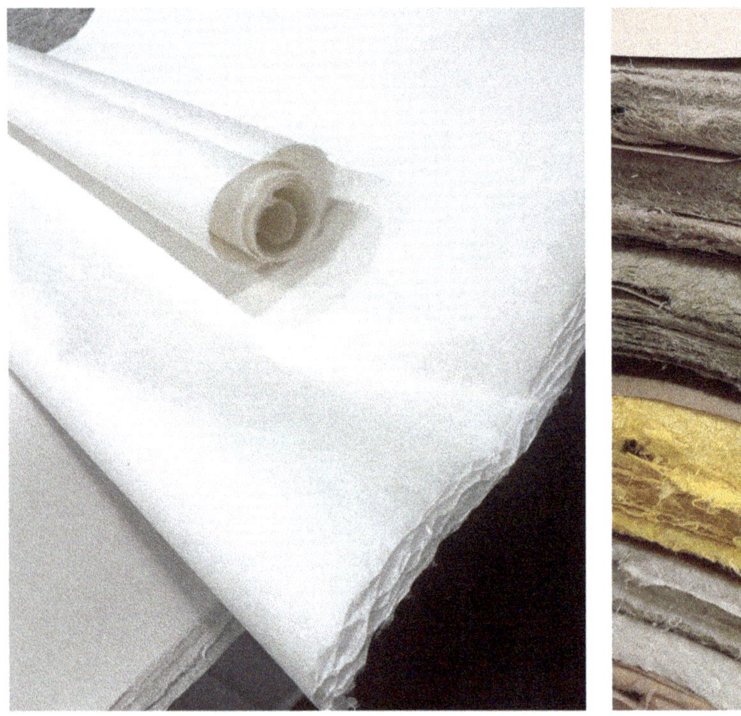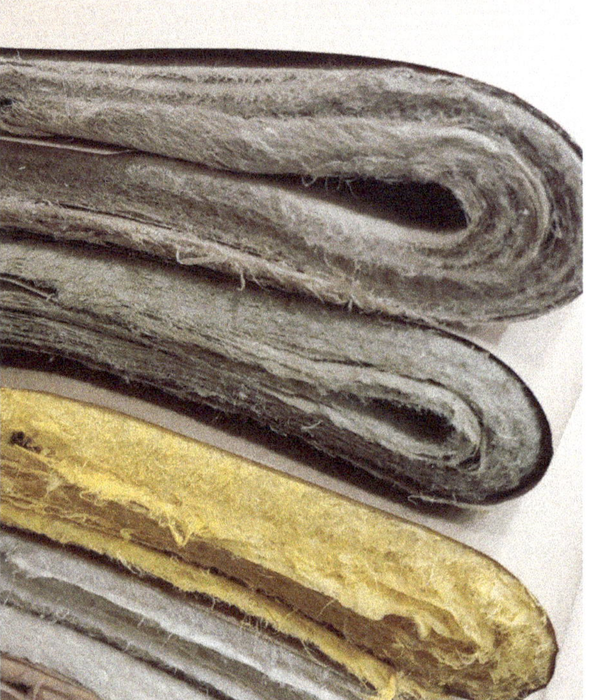

Hanji is a traditional Korean paper made from the fibers of the mulberry tree. It is categorized into single, double, or triple-layer papers based on thickness. For minhwa, single-layer or double-layer hanji is commonly used. It is important to store them in a dry place, away from moisture and dampness to preserve their quality.

Special pigments specifically made for Eastern Fine Arts are used in minhwa painting. These pigments come in various textures and types, evolving over the past hundreds of years.

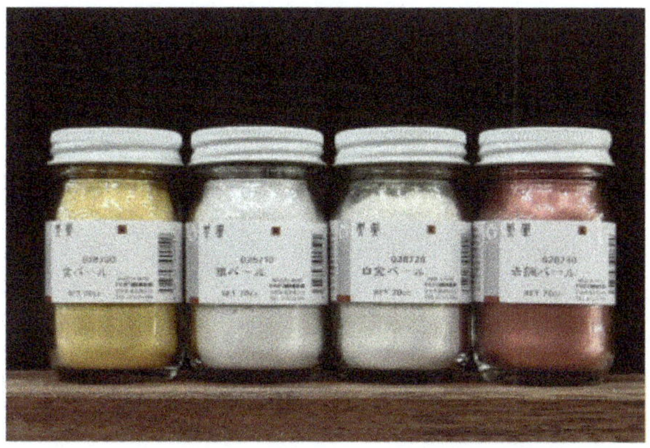

Stone Pigments (Seok-chae) are colors created by powdering natural minerals. Due to their coarse texture, these pigments must be filtered multiple times through a strainer when mixing. Seok-chae is typically packaged in small glass bottles and is known to be the rarest and most expensive type of pigment.

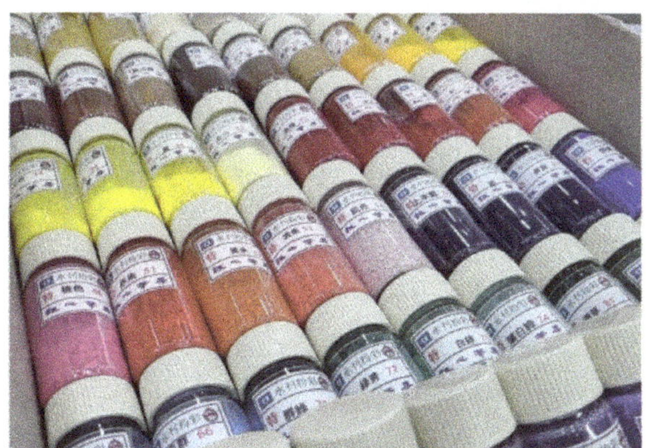

Powder Pigments (Boon-chae) are colors created by mixing fine earth with pigments. They have an ideal texture for detailed work, making them a favorite among serious minhwa artists. These pigments are typically sold in small glass bottles and can usually be found in art stores that specialize in Eastern Fine Arts.

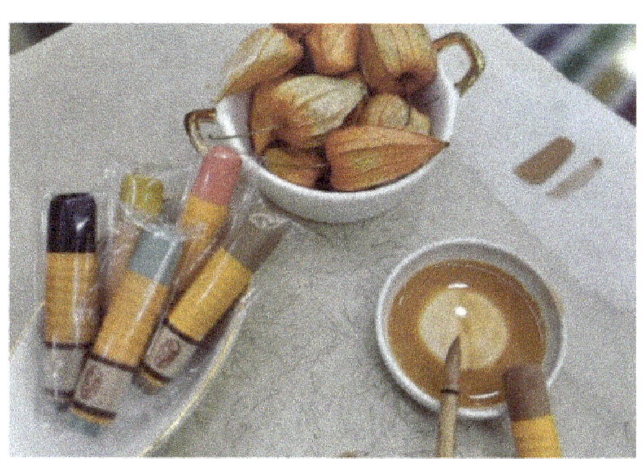

Stick Pigments (Boong-chae) are colors available in stick form, created by mixing boon-chae powder colors with agyo glue. Similar to the inkstone (meok) used in Eastern calligraphy, these sticks are ground on the inkstone to produce paint. They offer the clearest color quality.

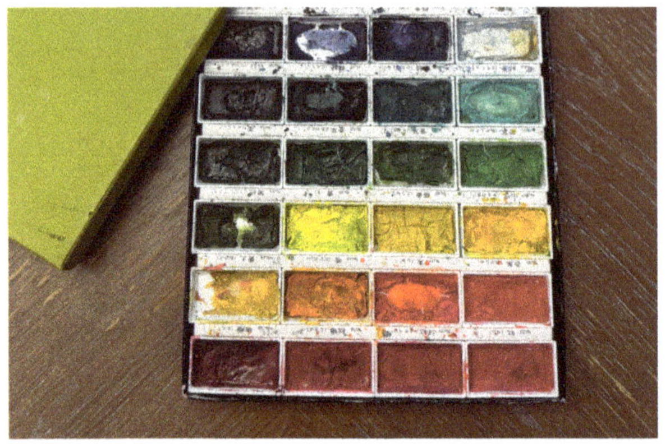

Pigment Palette (Anchae) are colors available in dried palette form created by pre-mixing powdered pigments. They are convenient to use and provide a finer texture compared to tube paints, resulting in a clearer and more transparent finish in paintings.

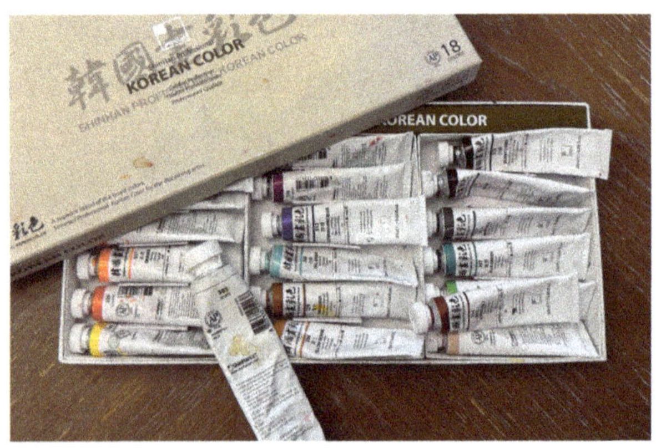

Tube paints are the most convenient option since no mixing or grinding is necessary.

In my Atlanta-based workshops, students prefer the Kuretake Gansai Tambi pigment palette (a Japanese brand) or ShinHan Korean Colors tube paints (a Korean brand). Both brands are commercially available in the USA and Europe, as well as on Amazon.

Brush

If possible, it is always best to use brushes made specifically for Eastern Fine Arts. For minhwa, the following types are required:

Flat Brush (pyeongbut): used for preparing the paper.

Blending Brush (barimbut): the most important brush in minhwa paintings. It is used in creating gradation and depth of colors. Short and firm brushes work best.

Coloring Brush (chaesaekbut): available in many different sizes and thickness. It is recommended to have several brushes on hand and use one brush per color.

Lining Brush (saepil): thinnest brush and used in the initial and final lining of the art.

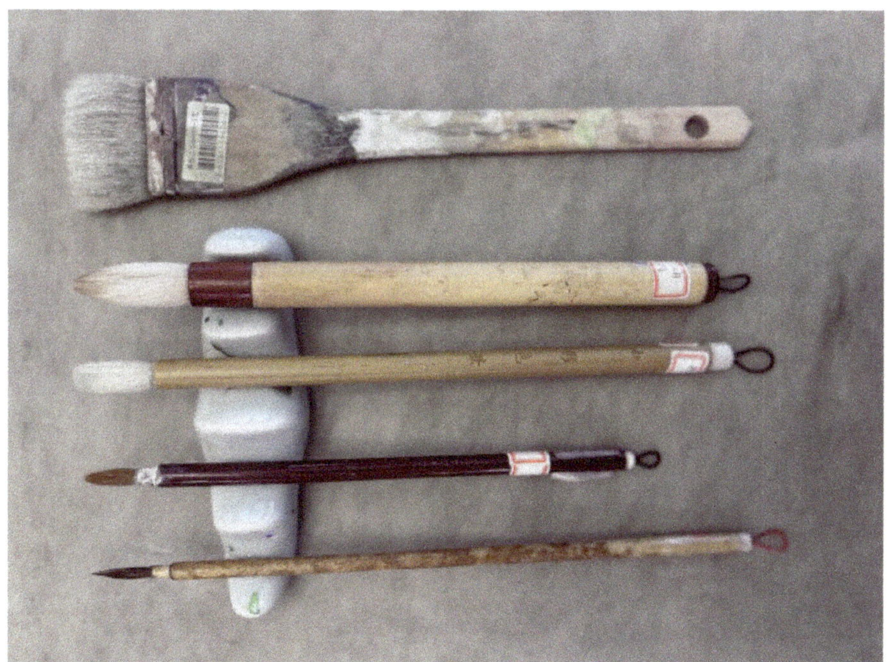

From top to bottom: flat brush, blending brush, two sizes of coloring brushes, and a lining brush.

Other Tools

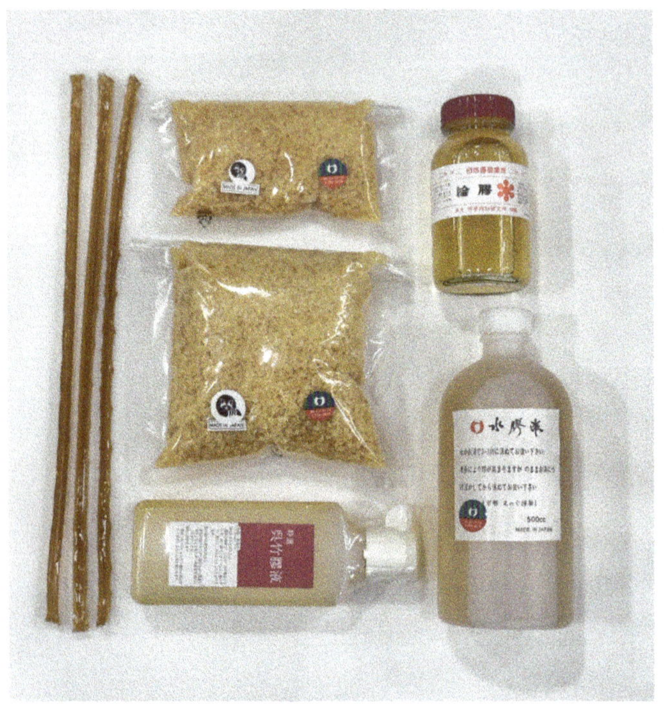 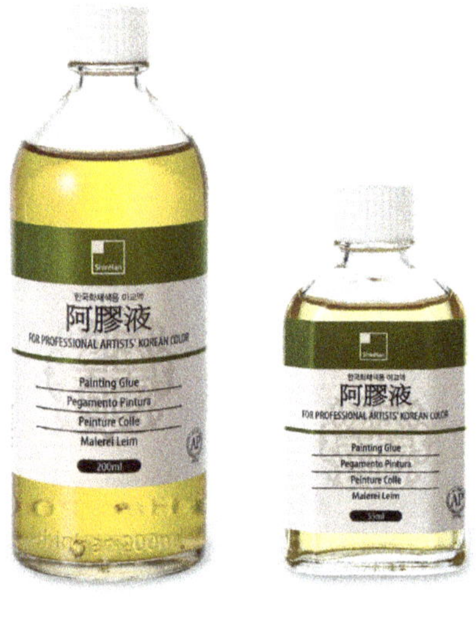

Agyo painting glue is an animal hide/collagen glue used as a binder in minhwa and other Eastern Fine Arts. It comes in various forms, including solid, granules, and liquid. The solid agyo is the most natural form, with minimal additives, resulting in the best viscosity. To use it, it should be melted in a double boiler, and any leftover melted agyo should be stored in the refrigerator and used within a few days. For beginners, the liquid form is a convenient and easy option. In my classes in Atlanta, we exclusively use liquid agyo glue.

NOTE: If agyo painting glue specific to Eastern Fine Arts is unavailable, you may substitute it with collagen glue used in distemper painting, which is available at fine arts stores in the West.

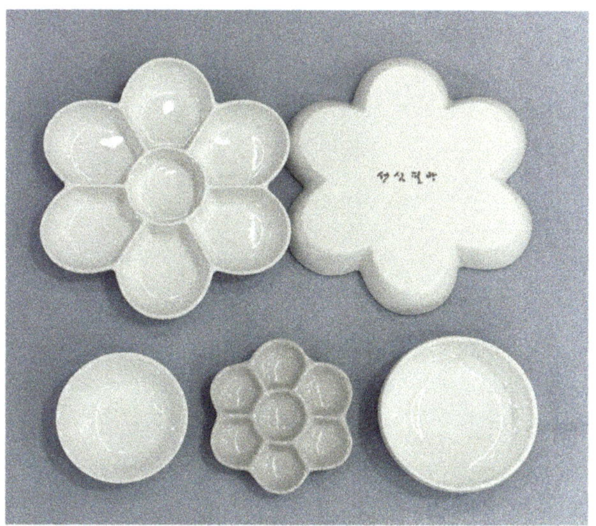
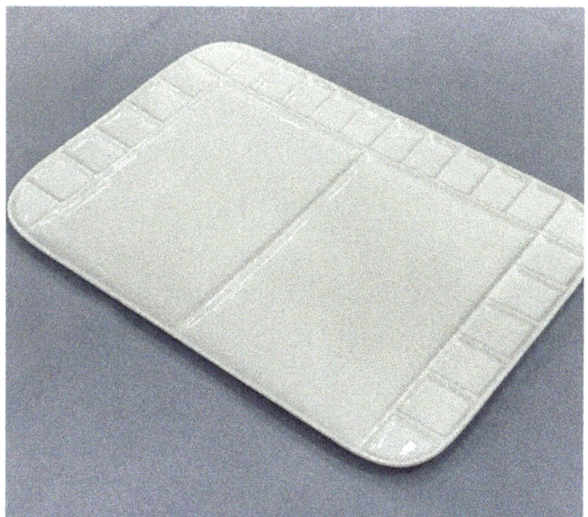

Palette: porcelain plates in various sizes can be used. There are also flower-shaped palettes designed specifically for Asian painting, but any type of palette is acceptable.

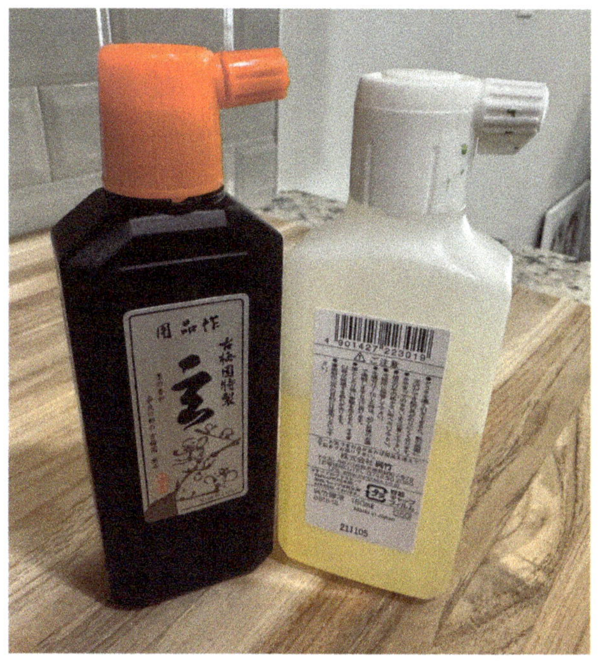

Liquid ink (meok mul) is a traditional black ink used in Asian calligraphy and painting. It is commonly used for initial design sketching or mixed with pigments to create darker shades. A small amount goes a long way. Traditionally, it was made by grinding an ink stick (meok) on an inkstone (byeoru), but today it is readily available in plastic bottles at art stores.

❀ Making a Minhwa Canvas ❀

Delicate hanji paper expands and contracts with changes in moisture, so securing the paper tightly onto the wooden panel helps create a smooth, even surface. We create a paper canvas using the wood panel and kraft paper. Lining paper acts as a barrier between the artwork and the wood panel. Any midweight paper, such as kraft paper, can be used provided it does not tear easily when wet.

Items Needed

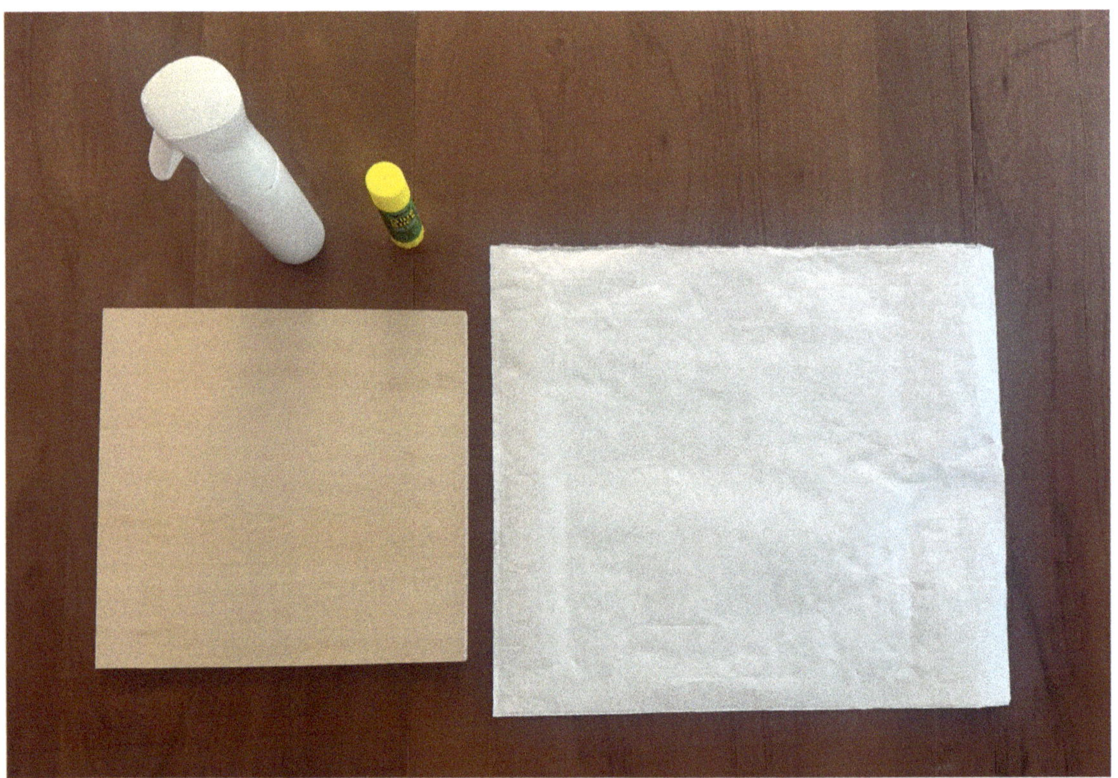

Wooden art board

Lining paper or kraft paper, cut to be 2 inches larger than the board on all edges

Glue stick

Water spray bottle

Knife or scissors

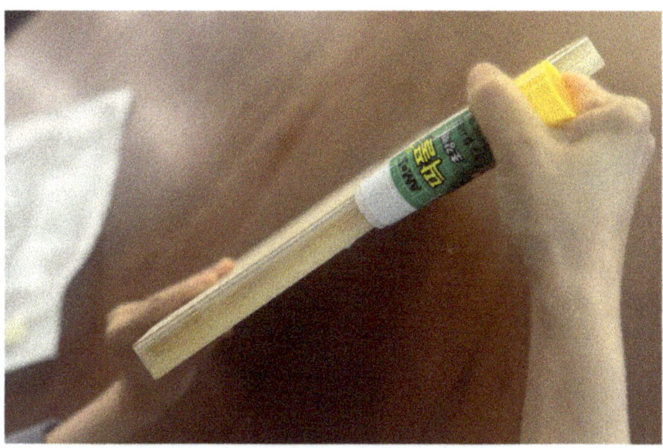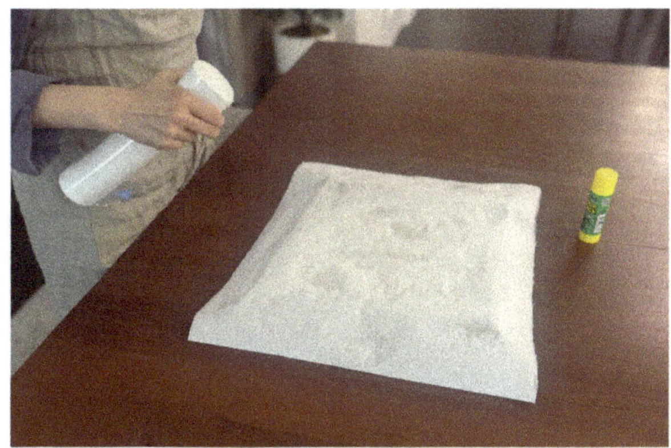

1. Using a glue stick, apply glue to the sides of the wood panel, being careful not to apply any glue to the painting surface. Ensure that you cover all the edges, paying special attention to the corners.

2. Next, place the lining paper on top of the board and spray it with plenty of water until it is damp but not soaked.

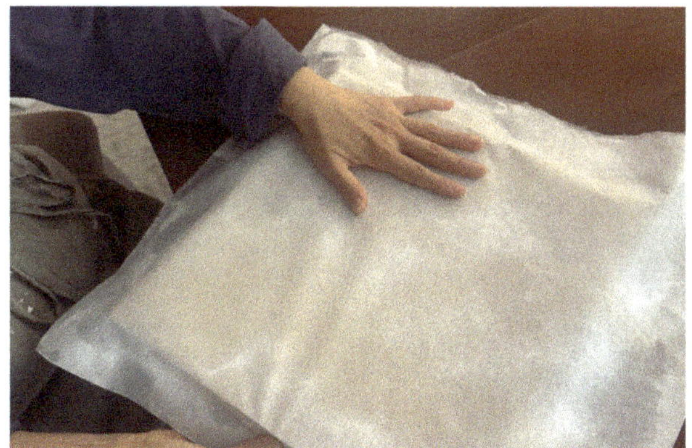

3. To stretch the paper without tearing it, gently pull it in four directions: first horizontally and then vertically. Once stretched, affix the paper to the glued edges of the board.

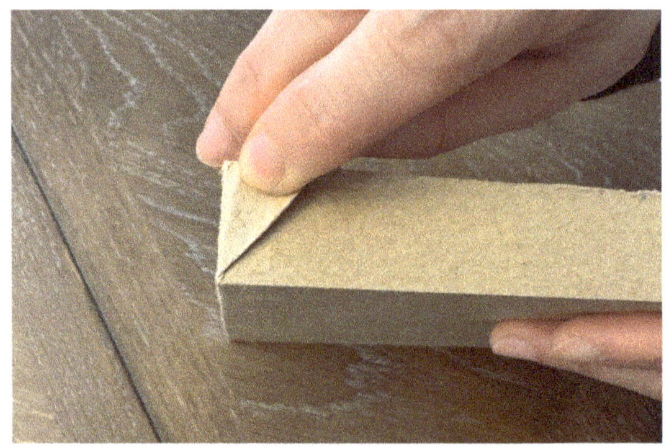 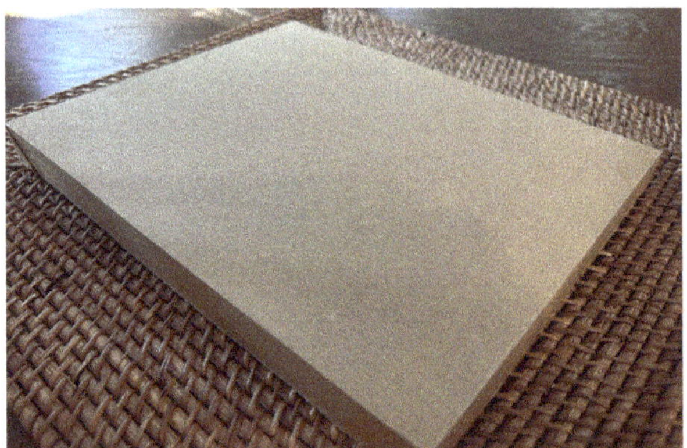

4. Fold the corners of the paper like the examples shown above and secure them with additional glue.

Try to apply the lining paper as flat and evenly as possible. As the paper dries completely, it will tighten and create a smooth surface.

❀ Paper Preparation ❀

Traditional hanji paper is very delicate and porous, so it needs to be treated with a special solution to endure the multiple layers of colors and brushstrokes required for minhwa painting. You can find pre-treated papers, known as batangji or agyoji, available in a variety of colors at specialty fine arts stores in Korea. However, it is more cost-effective to create your own treated paper using the methods outlined in this book.

AGYO SOLUTION TREATMENT

The baselayer solution made with agyo glue is essential in minhwa painting, as it prevents colors from spreading and soaking into the delicate paper.

Items Needed

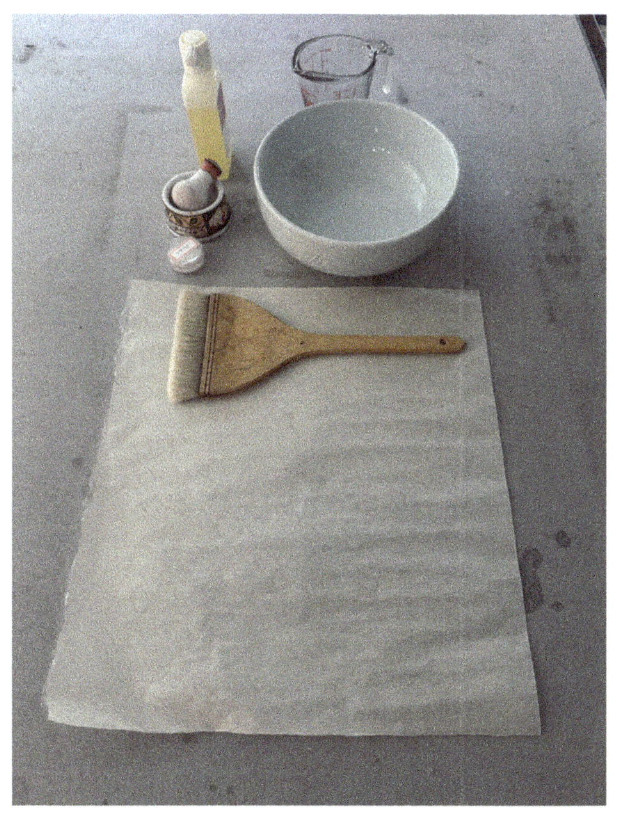

Hanji sheets (single-layer or double-layer)

Liquid agyo

Finely ground alum powder

Heated water (hot but not boiling)

A flat brush.

MAKING AGYO SOLUTION

Combine 100 ml of liquid agyo with 300 ml of hot water and add 1/8 tsp of finely ground alum powder. Stir well to mix.

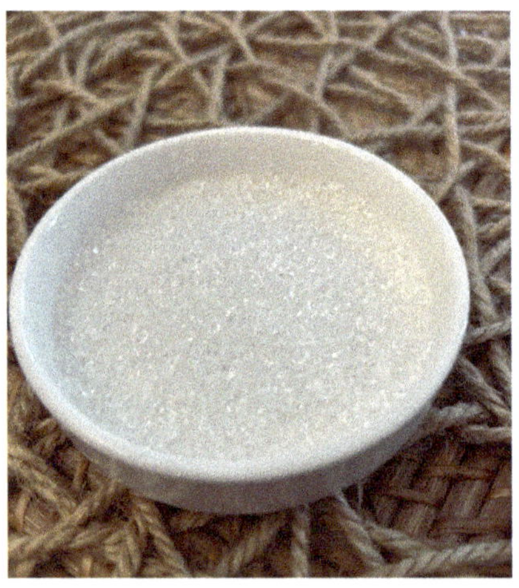
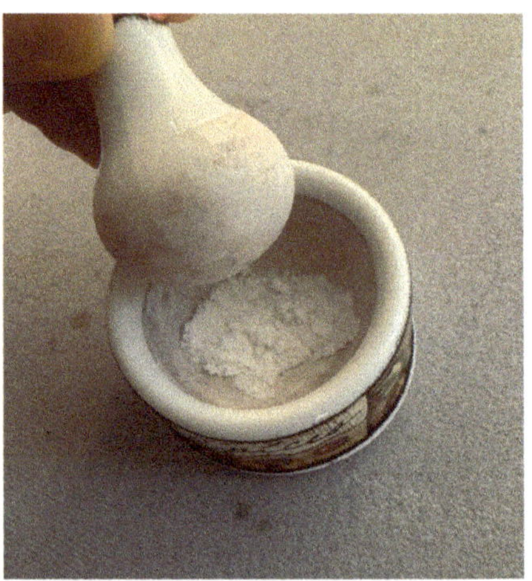

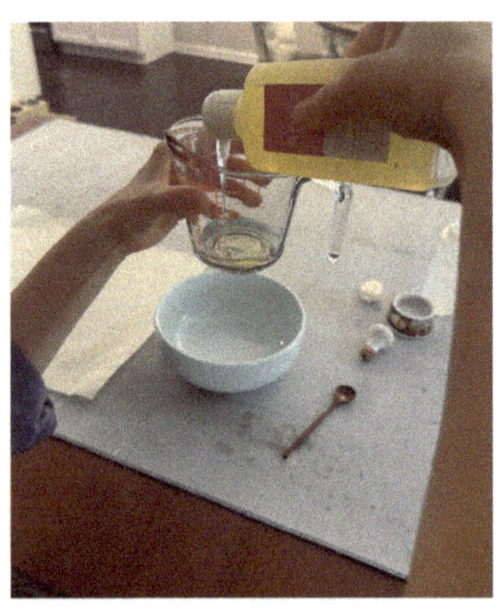
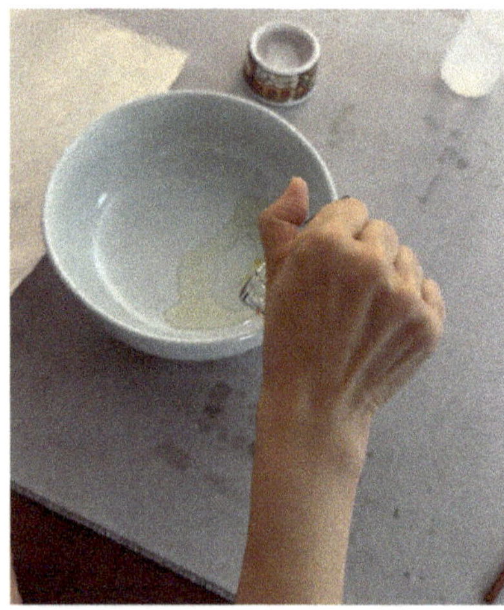
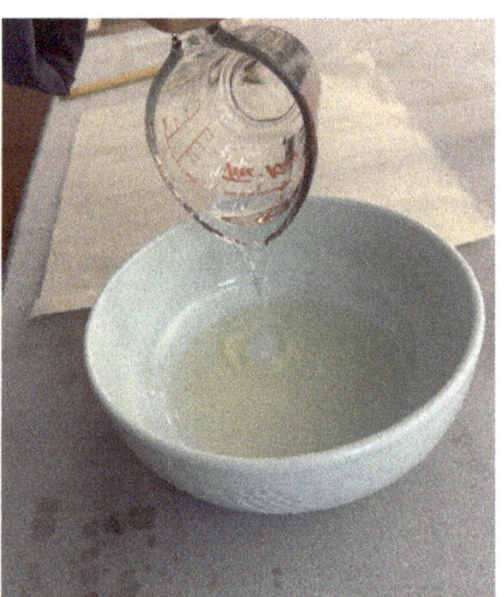

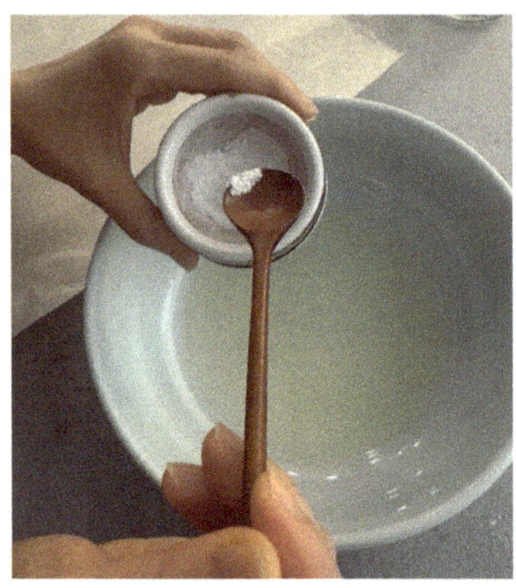
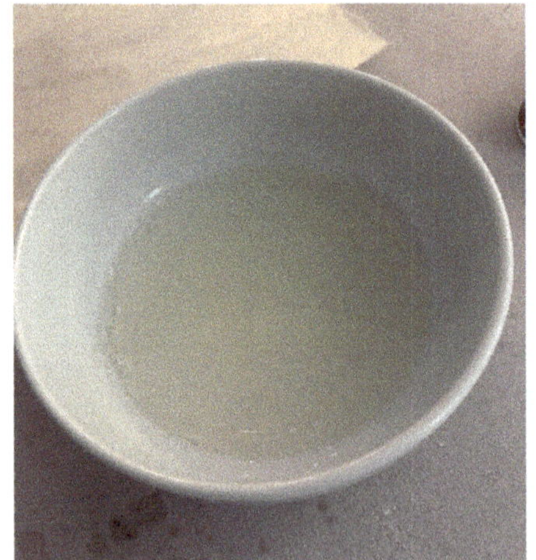

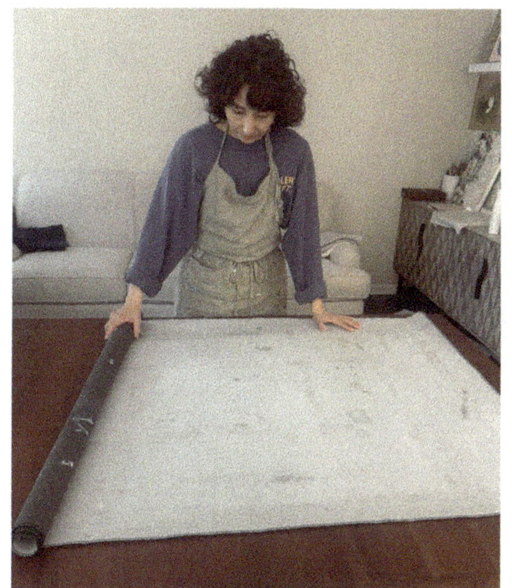 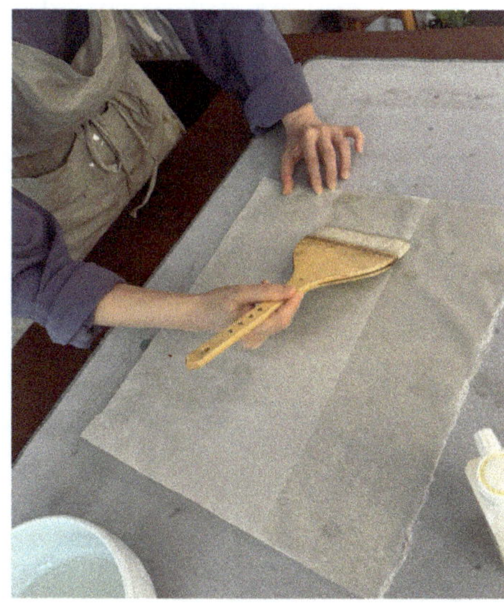 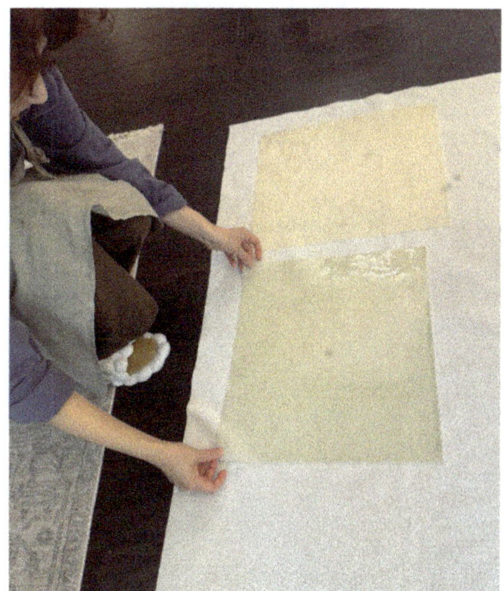

1. To protect the table, cover it with a fabric.

2. Next, lay a sheet of hanji paper flat, ensuring the smooth side is facing up, while the textured side remains down.

3. Using a flat brush, apply the agyo solution evenly in one direction. Use minimal brush strokes and apply slowly and mindfully to ensure the entire surface of the paper is covered with the baselayer. Holding the flat brush sideways, almost parallel to the paper, can help achieve a more uniform application.

4. Once the application is complete, carefully move the prepared paper to the drying area. Make sure the drying area is ready for use.

5. Allow the paper to dry completely.

To test if the baselayer has been applied correctly, spray some clean water onto the fully dried paper. If water droplets form and do not soak into the paper, the application has been successful.

COLORING THE PAPER

Once fully dried, the treated paper is ready for minhwa painting, typically starting with a simple white background. Many artists prefer to color the paper in light, neutral shades that complement the artwork.

For centuries, various natural ingredients have been used to dye paper. Dried berries, flowers, and teas are popular choices. Additionally, different mixtures of pigments and ink water can create a wide range of colors.

These colors are then combined with the agyo solution (prepared on page 12), and applied on top of the fully dried, baselayer-treated paper.

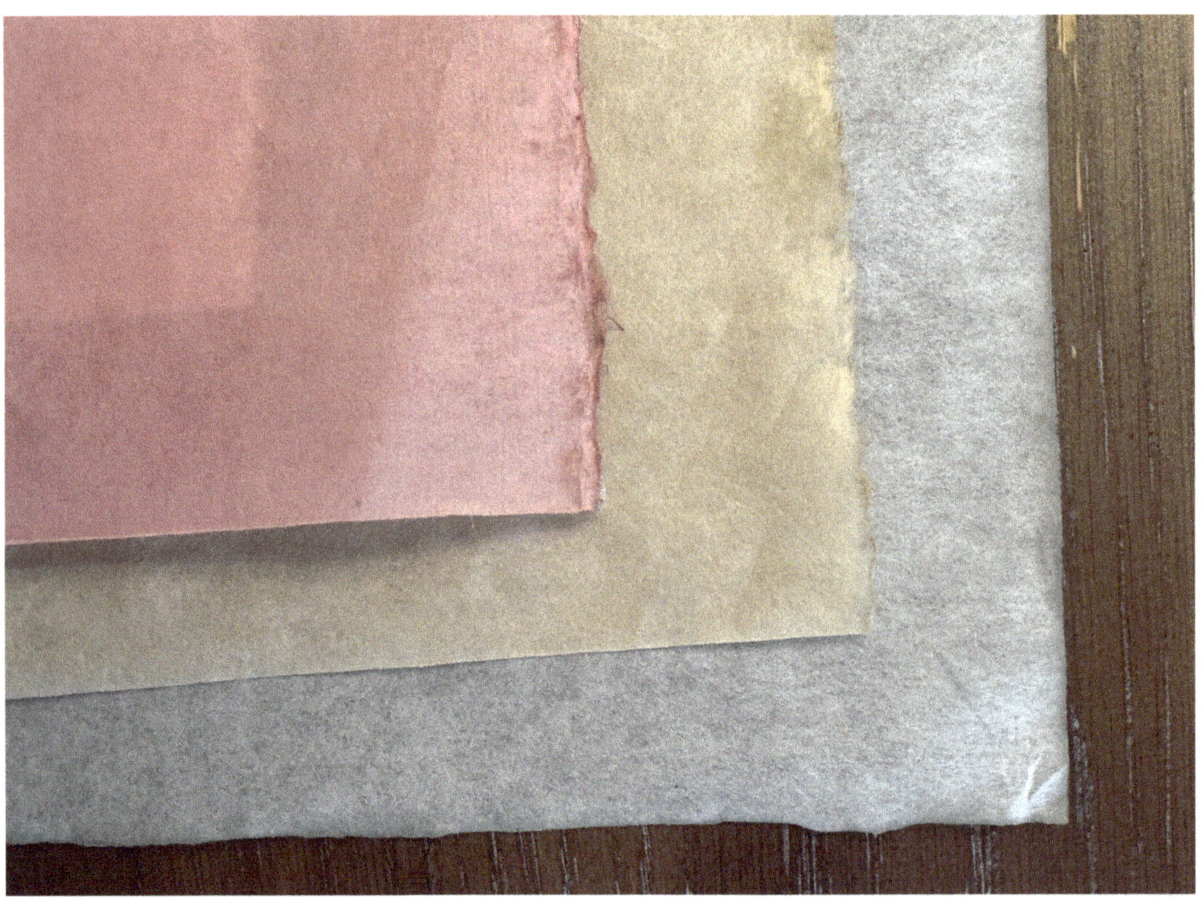

Pink-, brown-, and blue-dyed papers. See the next page for how to mix these colors.

Please note that the colors will be diluted when mixed with the agyo solution, resulting in a lighter background color.

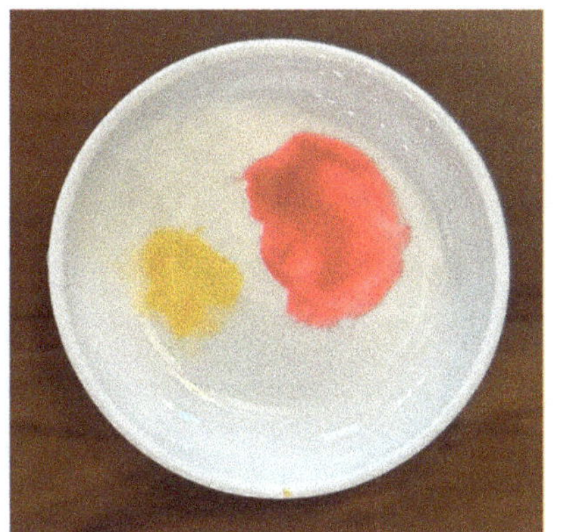 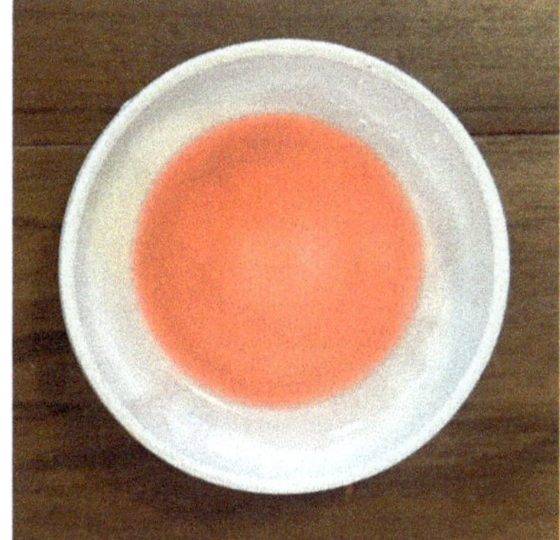

Pink

Kuretake colors: Rose Madder Deep (34) + Yellow Ochre (44)
ShinHan colors: Carnmin2 (339) + Yellow Ochre (304)

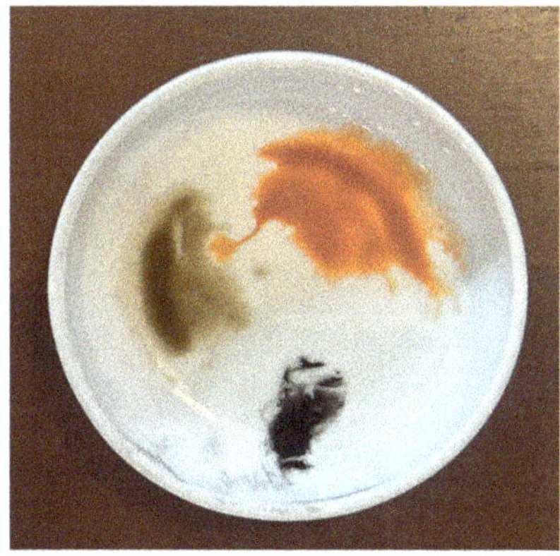 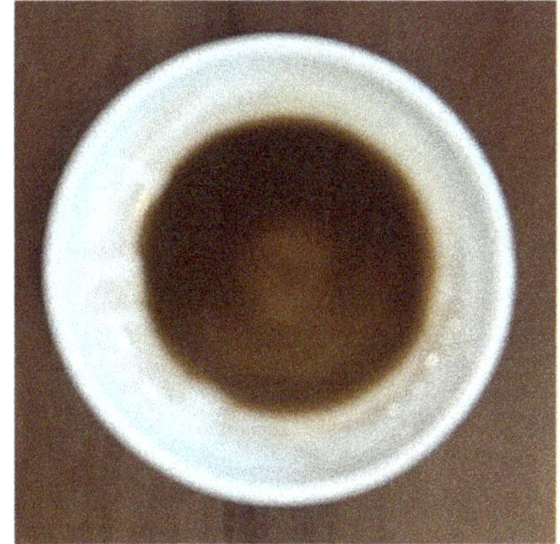

Brown

Kuretake colors: Burnt Sienna (46) + Raw Umber Deep (47) + a drop of inkwater
ShinHan colors: Burnt Sienna (303) + Burnt Umber (318) + a drop of inkwater

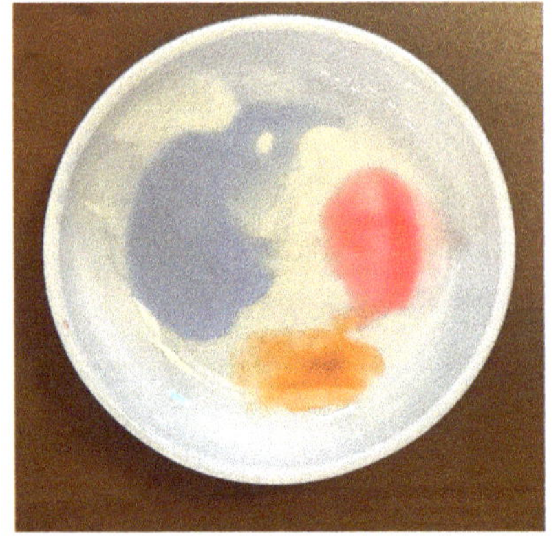 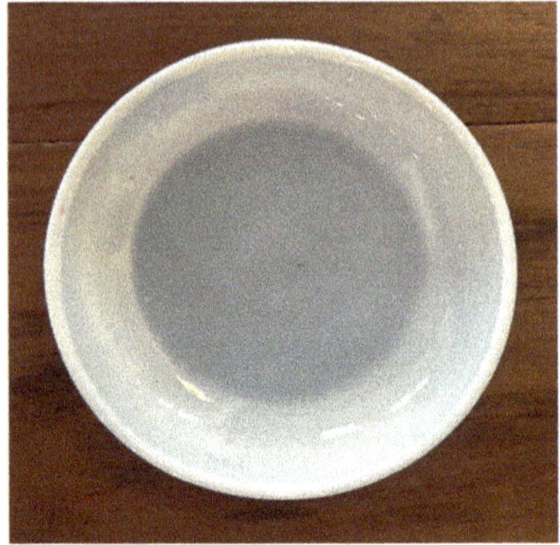

Kuretake colors: Ultramarine Pale (61) + Rose Madder Deep (34) + Burnt Sienna (46)
ShinHan colors: Purple Blue Pale (315) + Carmin2 (339) + Burnt Sienna (303)

NOTE: Since the traditional process of applying baselayer coating, fully drying the paper, then applying color dye and drying again can be complicated for beginners, I introduce a time-saving cheat method. You can combine two steps into one by mixing colors directly into the baselayer solution and applying it once.

1. Combine 50 ml of liquid agyo with 150 ml of hot water (using a 1:3 ratio).

2. Add 1/8 teaspoon of finely ground alum powder.

3. Mix the colors into the solution.

4. Apply the mixture with a flat brush and let it dry completely.

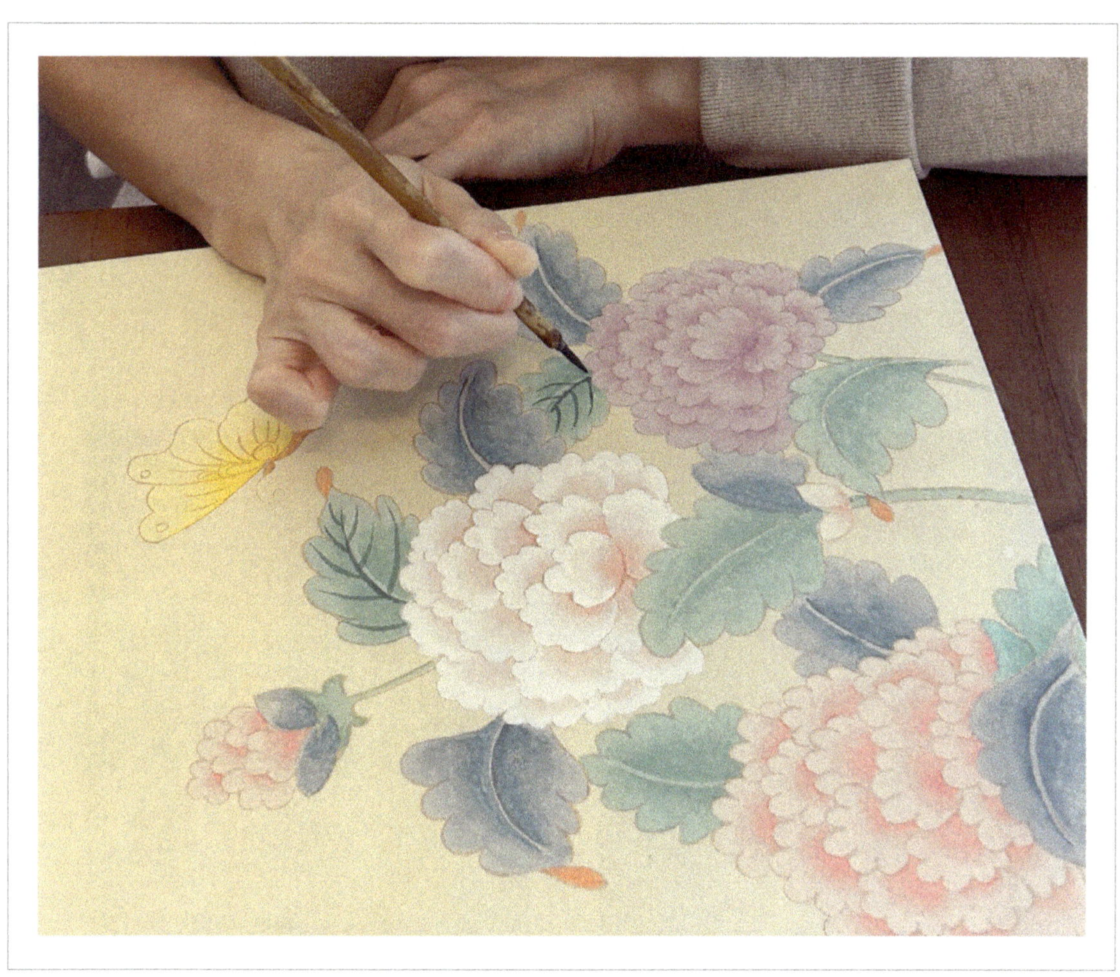

❀ Outlining the Design ❀

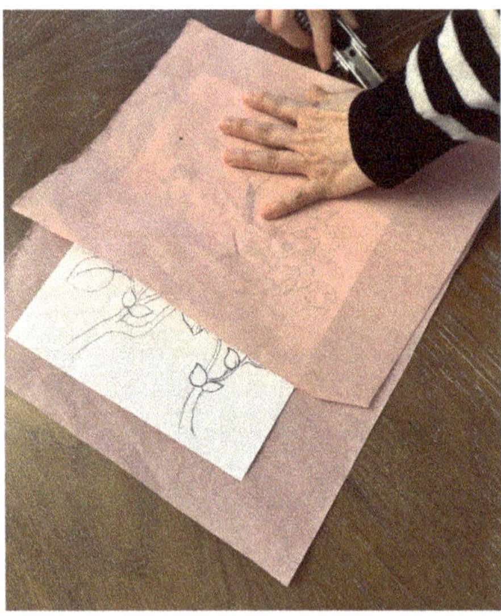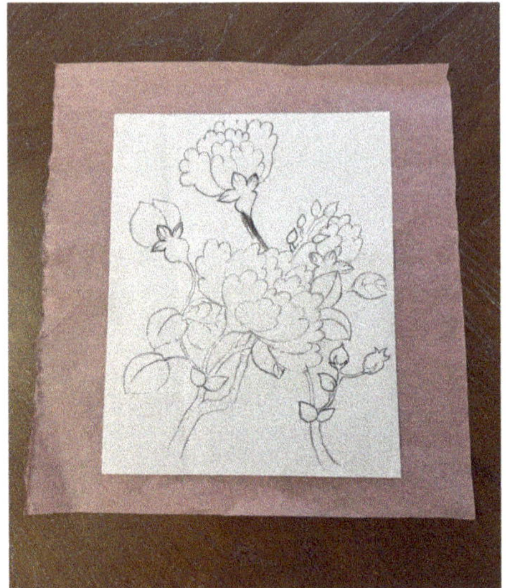

1. Cut the treated hanji paper to a size that is two inches larger on all sides than your artwork.

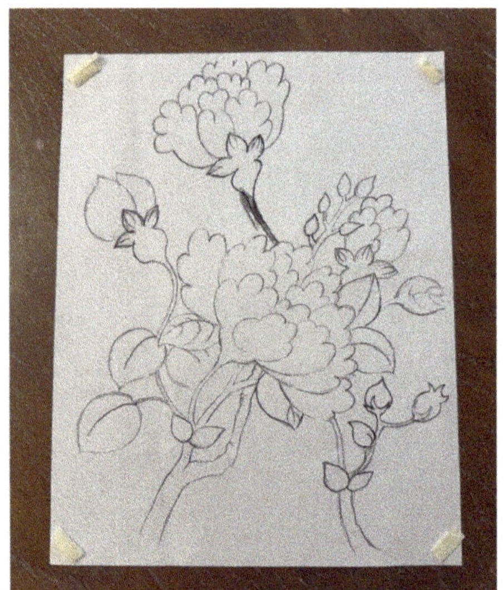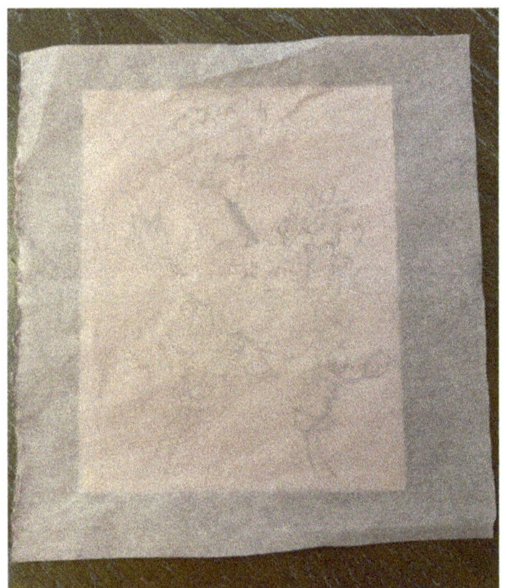

2. Use a few pieces of masking tape to secure the corners of the artwork. Place the hanji paper on top of the artwork, securing it in place.

NOTE: Hanji has a smooth side and a rough side; you should make sure the smooth side is facing up. Since hanji is thin and somewhat transparent, you should be able to see the outline of the design underneath.

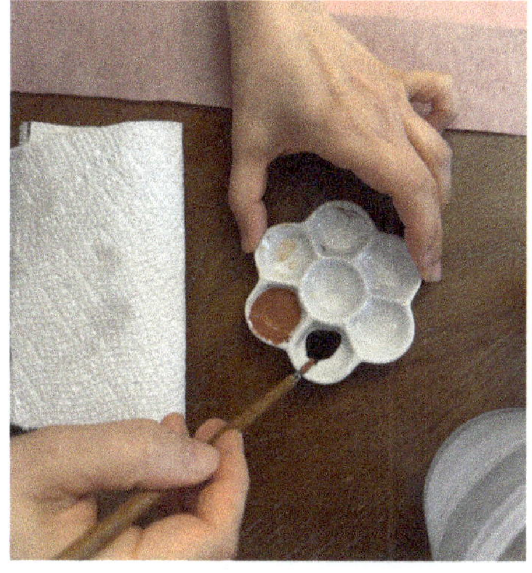
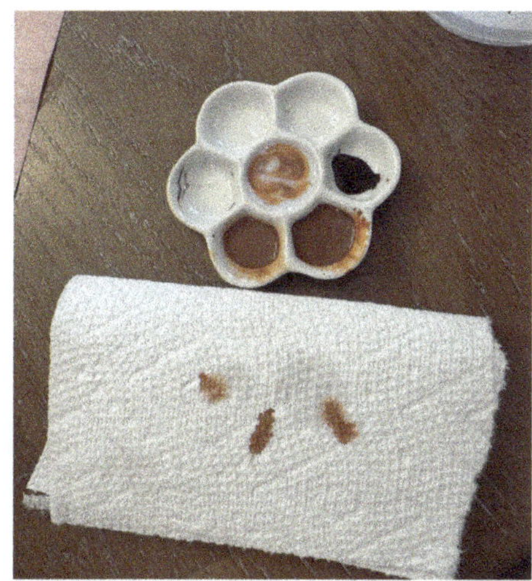

3. Mix Burnt Sienna (or brown) color with a few drops of inkwater and water. The inkwater will darken the color and increase its durability. Add a few drops of *liquid agyo* to the mixture to help prevent the color from spreading.

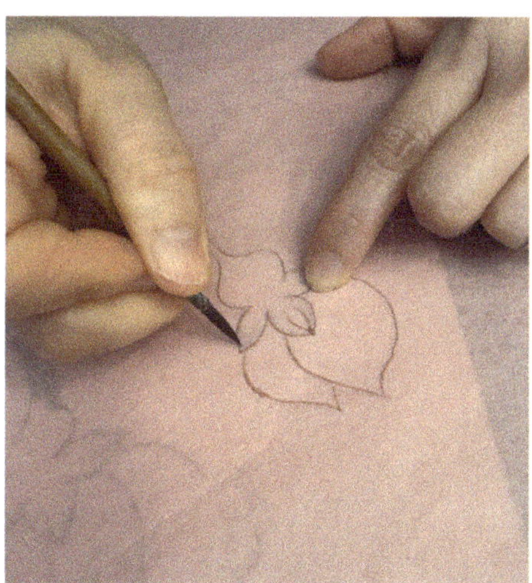
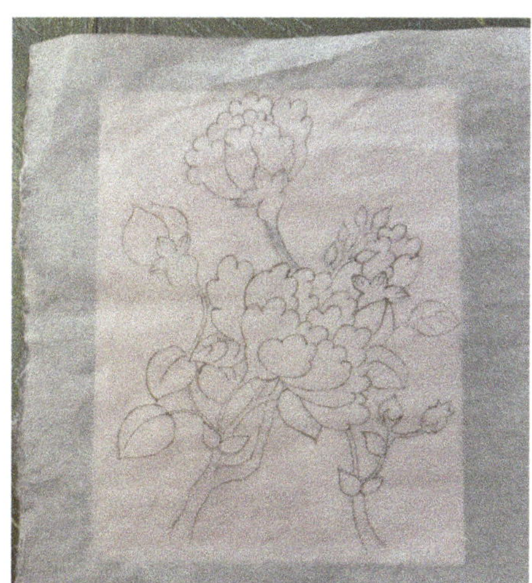

4. Using a lining brush, carefully trace the design directly onto the paper. Be sure to dab off any excess paint on a towel to keep the outline light.

5. Once you have finished outlining, gently remove the tape and set the design aside for future use.

❀ Mounting the Outlined Artwork ❀

You can attach the artwork to a prepared paper canvas using the following steps.

1. Apply glue to the edges of the paper canvas.

2. Spray water on the back side of the artwork (the rough side of the paper).

3. Stretch the damp paper in four directions and secure it firmly onto the canvas.

4. Fold the corners and adhere them well using a glue stick.

5. Trim off any excess paper.

Your artwork is now mounted on the paper canvas and ready for coloring.

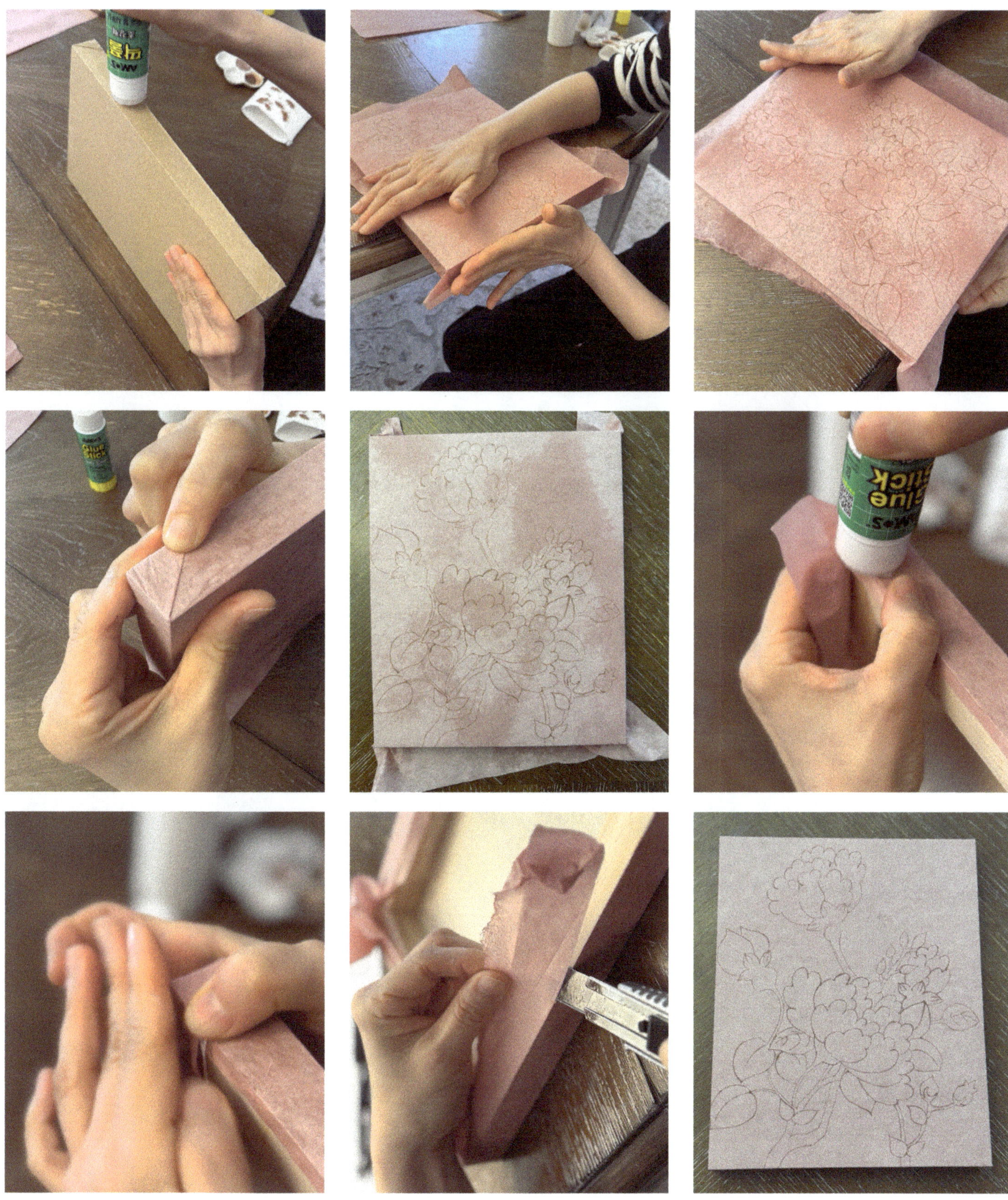

❀ Coloring — Mindful Layers ❀

Instead of using darker colors or thicker strokes to depict depth and shadows in the painting, minhwa employs a slow and mindful layering technique called barim-jil. This method allows for subtle color gradation and depth.

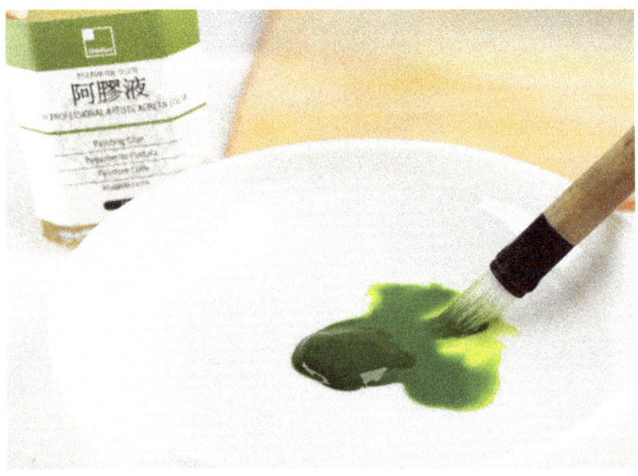

To achieve the right viscosity and durability for layering, all prepared colors are mixed with a few drops of glue. The consistency of the paint, when mixed with water, should resemble that of milk. After achieving this consistency, add a few drops of liquid agyo to the mixture.

First Layer (Light Colors)

Colors are applied in layers, starting from the lightest to the darkest. After applying the first layer of the lightest color, ensure you wait for it to dry completely.

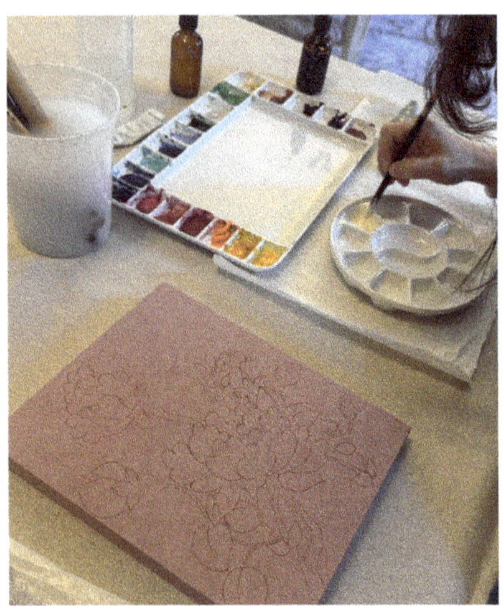
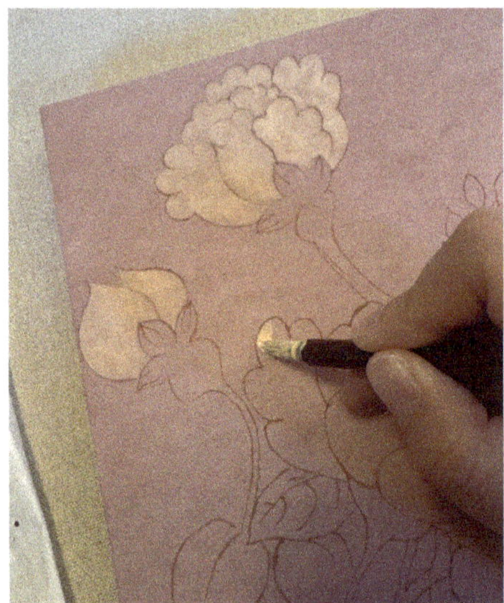
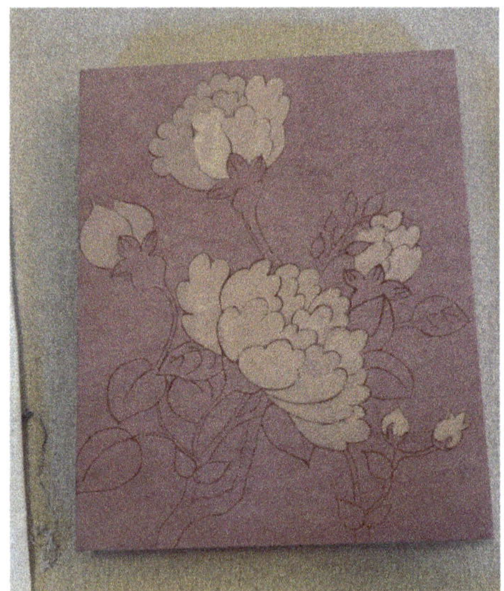

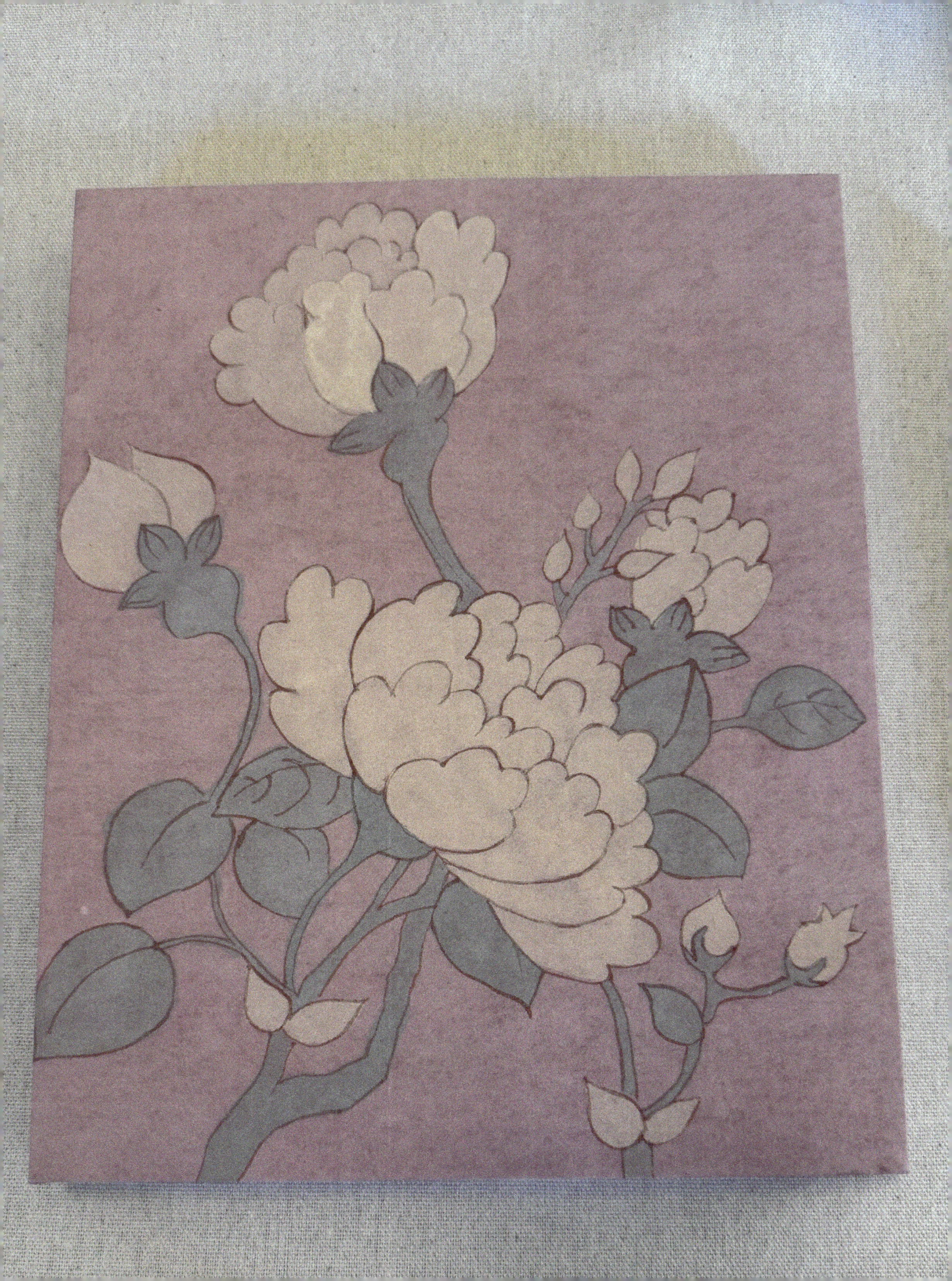

Once the first color layer is fully dry, apply the second layer of color using a coloring brush on the areas that need darker shades. While the paint is still wet, use a blending brush to blend and soften the edges, creating a natural gradient and depth.

Before applying new colors, use a paper towel or rag to blot excess paint from the coloring brush. Ensure that the brush or towel is not too wet, as this can cause the paint to spread outside the lines.

The blending brush should be damp but not dripping. Squeeze out all excess water from the brush to effectively use the barim technique.

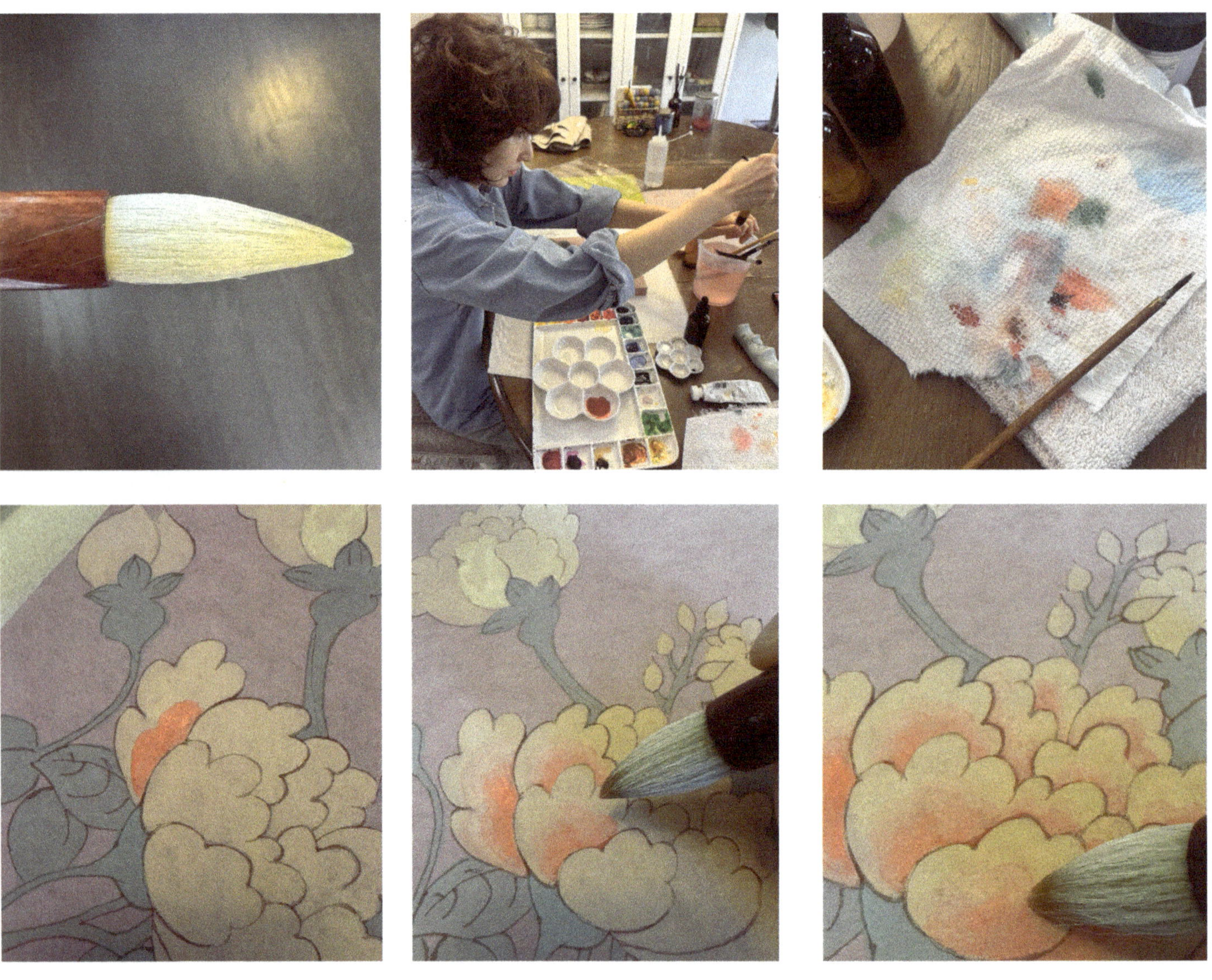

NOTE: Use tiny circular motions to blend and blur.

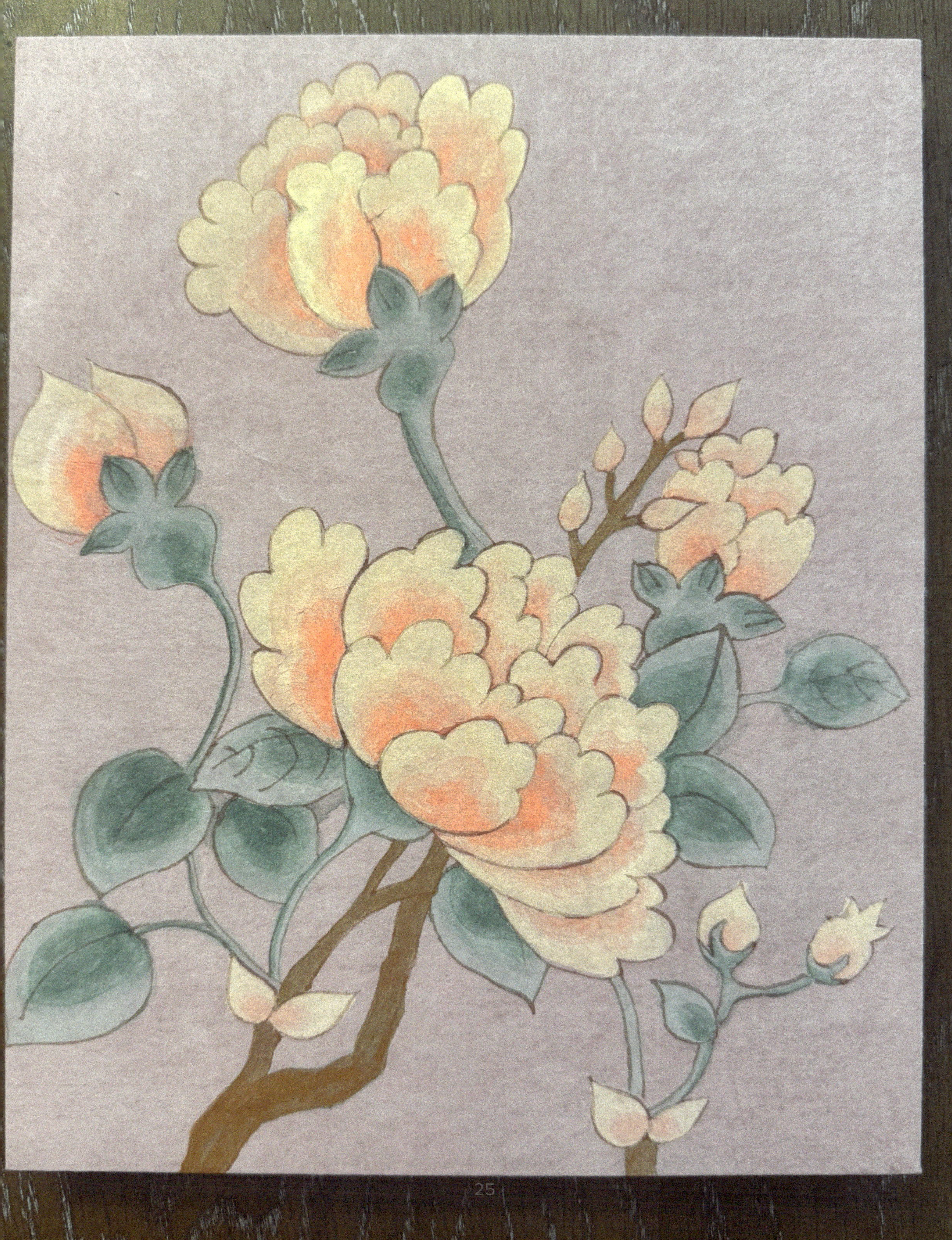

Third Layer (Dark Colors)

Dark colors matching from the second layers are applied to show depth and detail. Repeat applying the color with the coloring brush, then blending the edges with the blending brush.

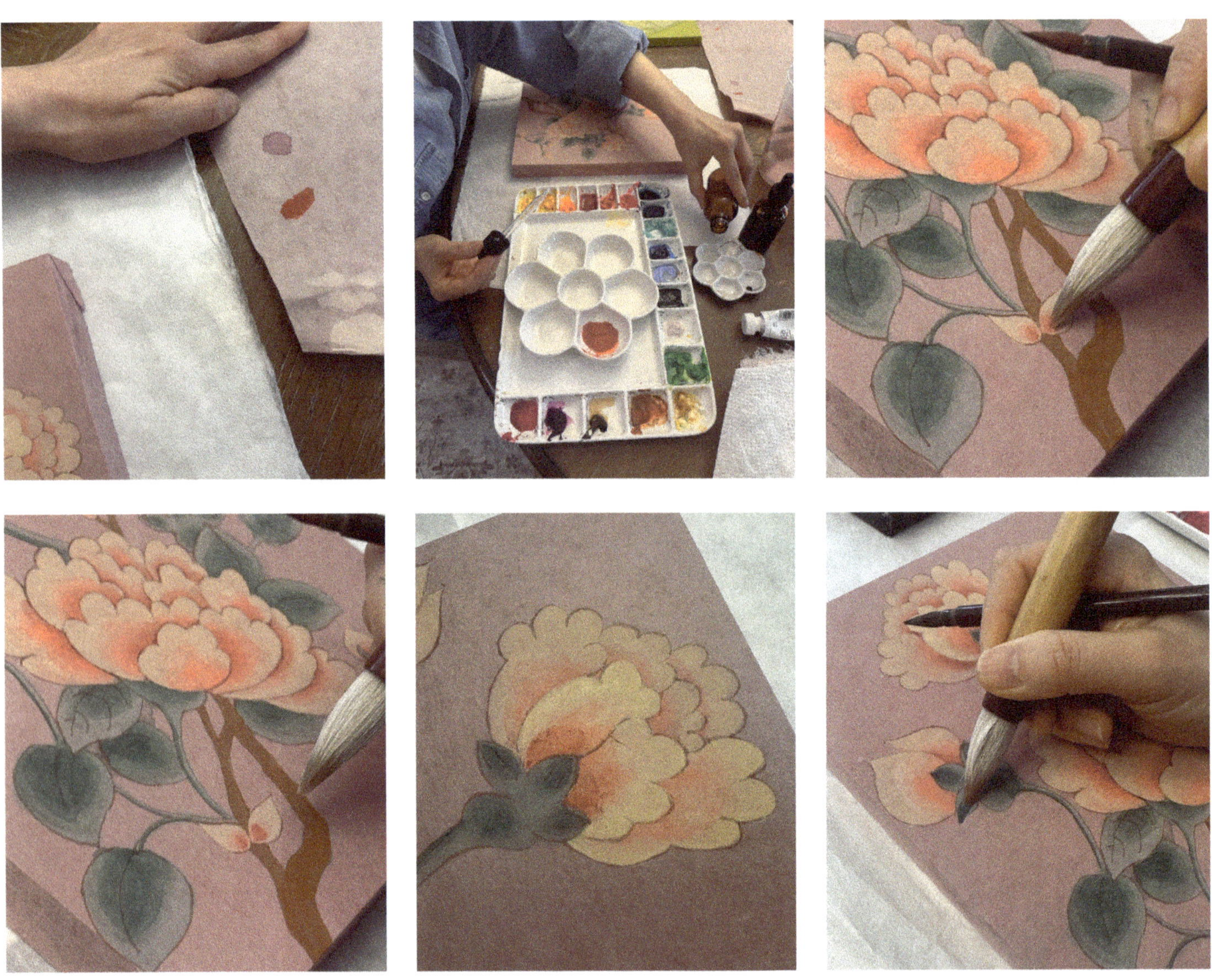

NOTE: It is easier to hold the coloring brush and the blending brush in the same hand.

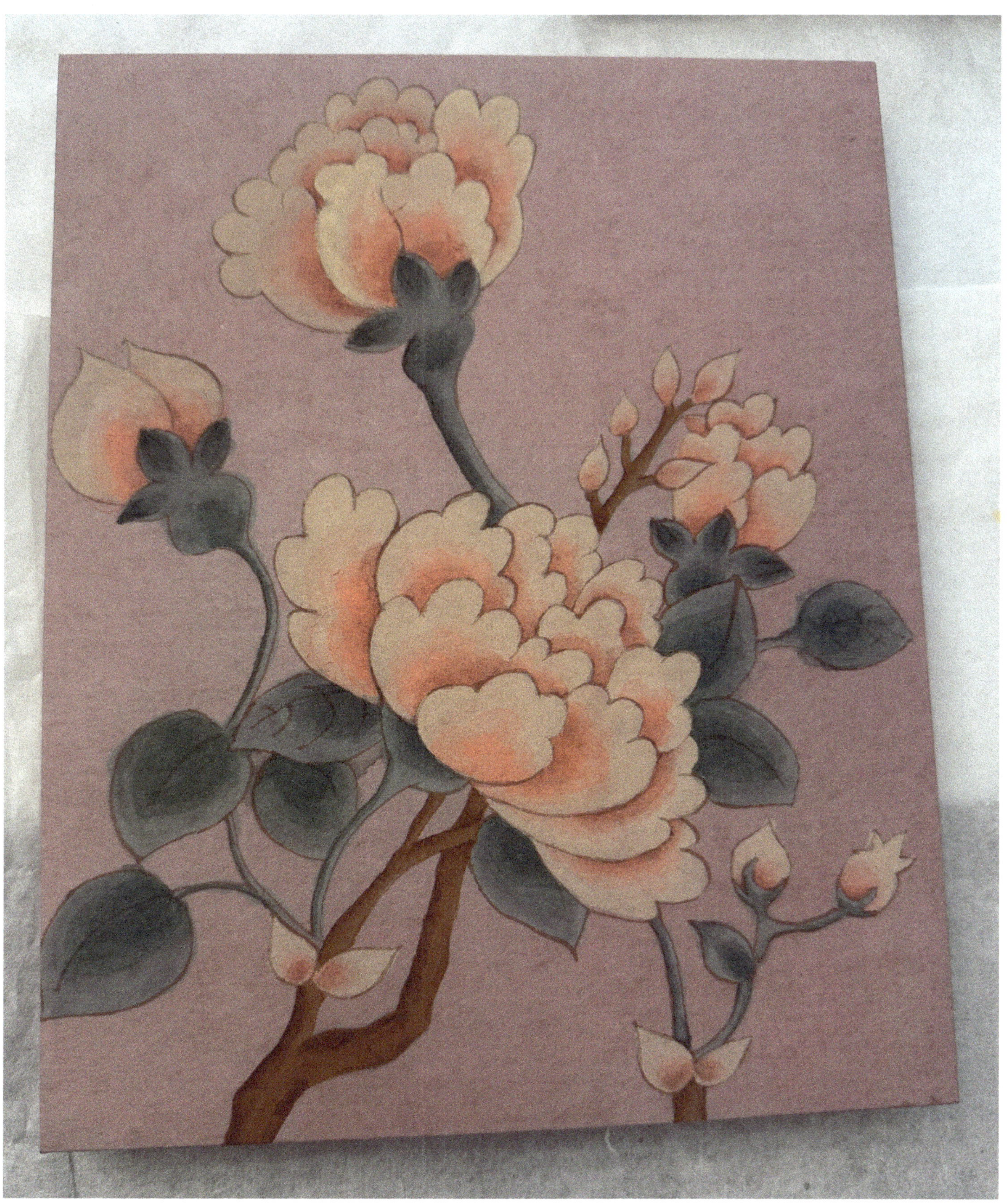

Fourth Layer (Lightest or Darkest Colors)

In this example, the fourth layer was applied using the lightest color to complement the actual peonies' light hues. However, depending on the artwork, this layer could also utilize the darkest colors. For minhwa, I recommend that my students use a minimum of three or four layers of color. In my own projects, it is common for me to apply seven or eight layers of barim. Ultimately, the decision on the number of layers is up to you.

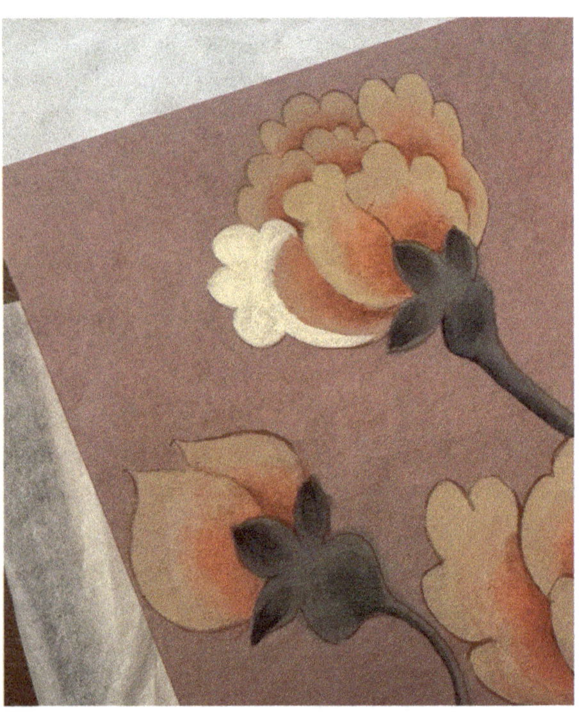 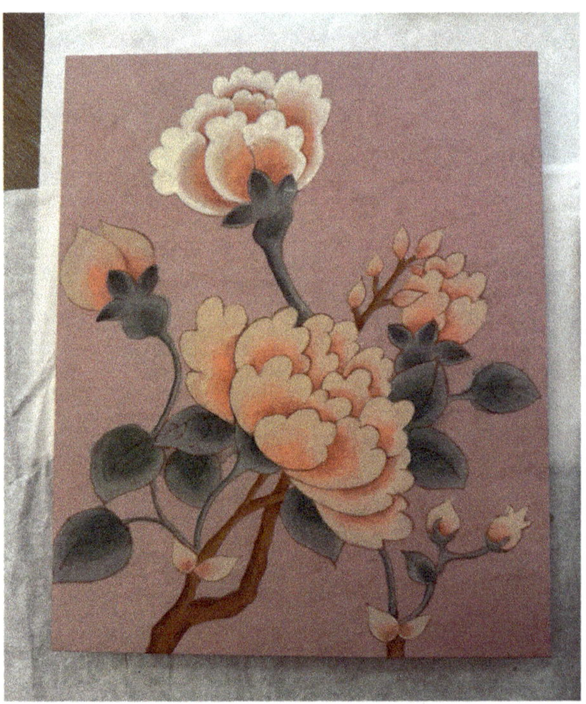

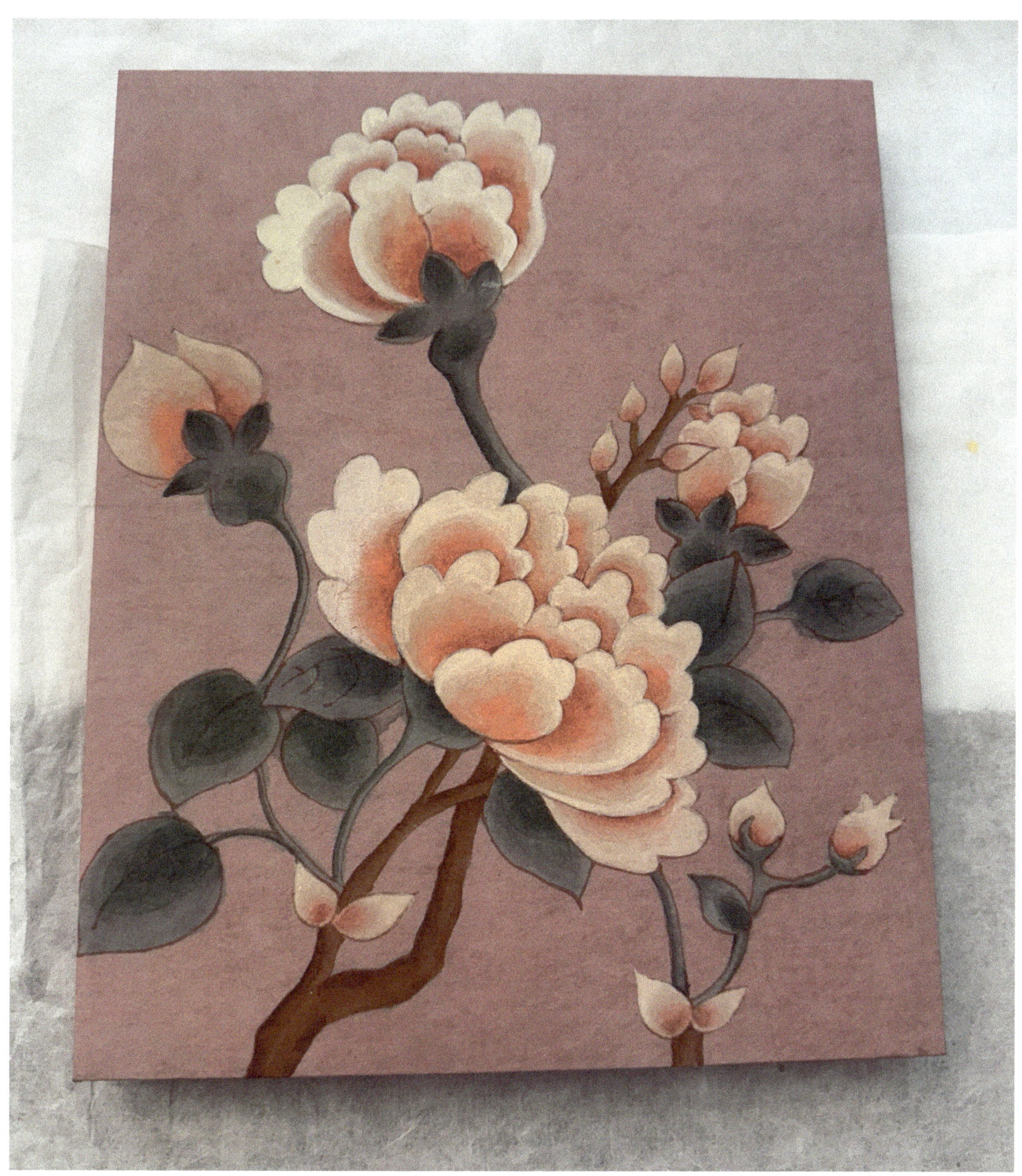

❀ Finishing Touch ❀

Use the darkest colors. Utilize a lining brush to add the final outlines and details to the painting. Incorporate any decorative elements as needed.

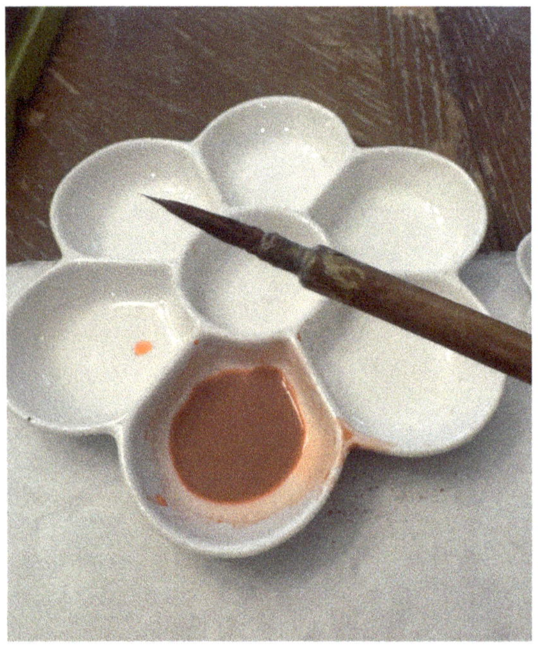

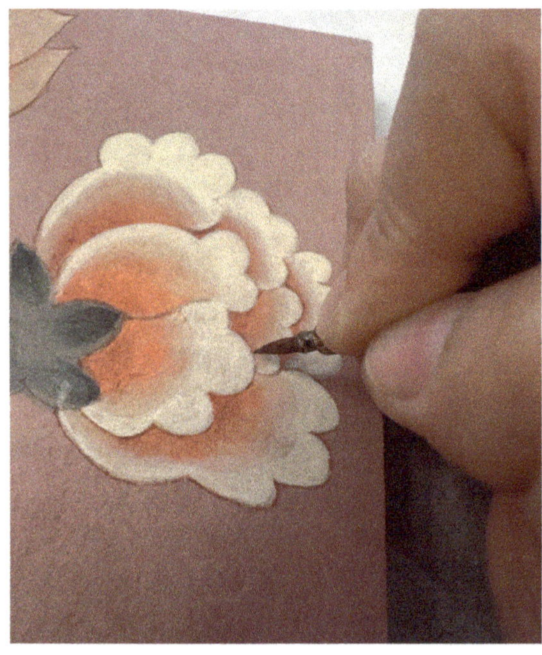

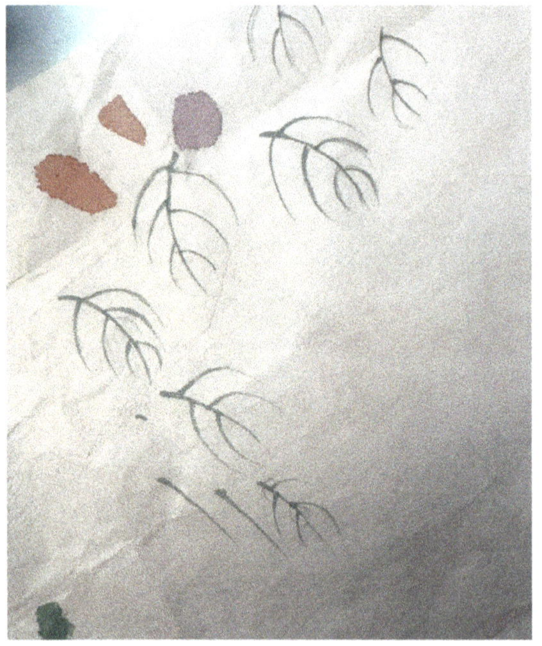

NOTE: Since it's hard to make corrections in the final stage, practice final details on a scrap paper a few times to ensure you are comfortable with how they will look.

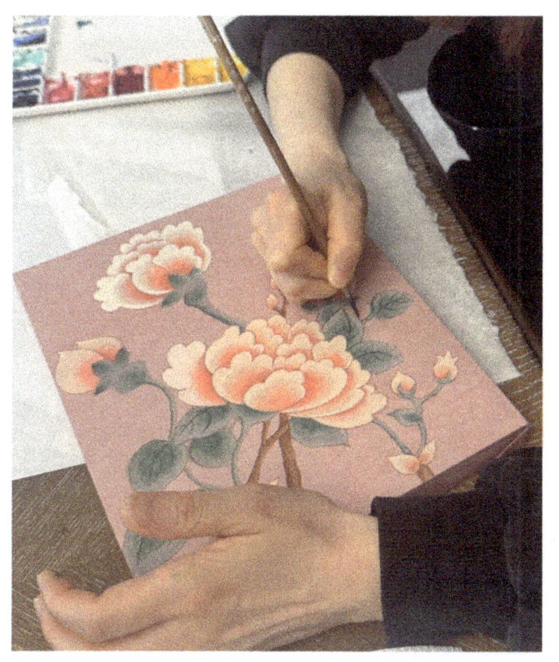

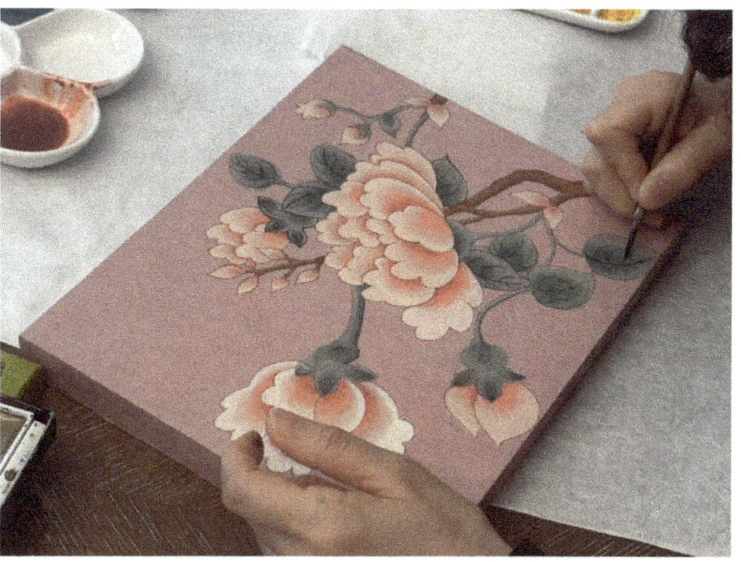

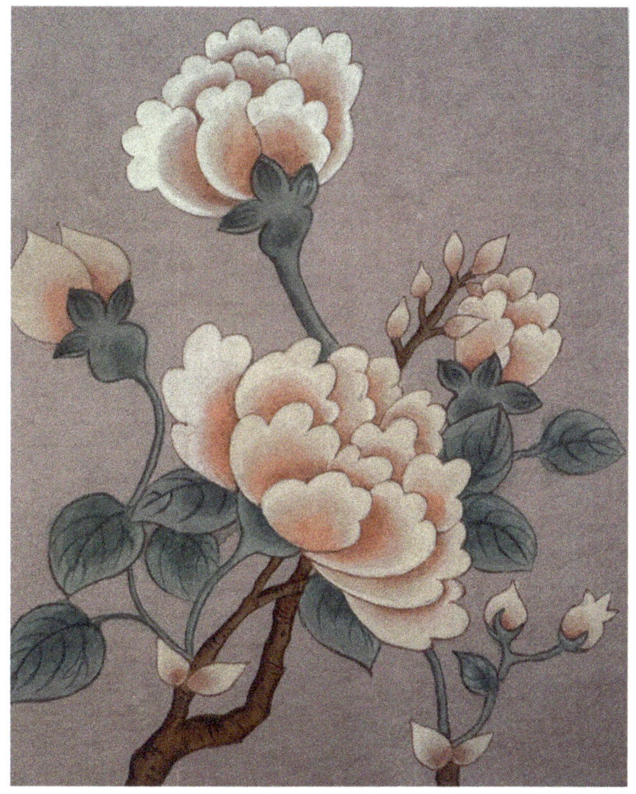

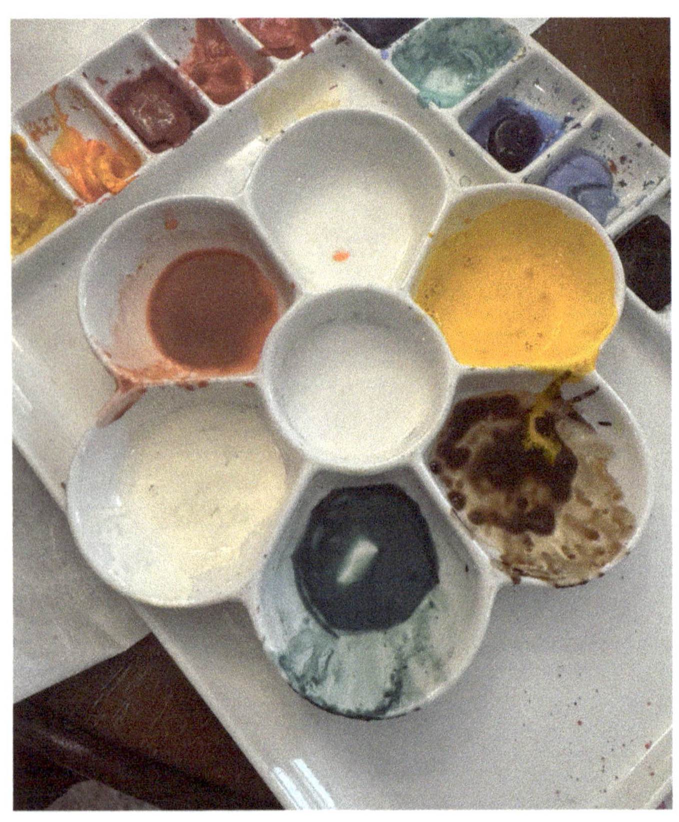
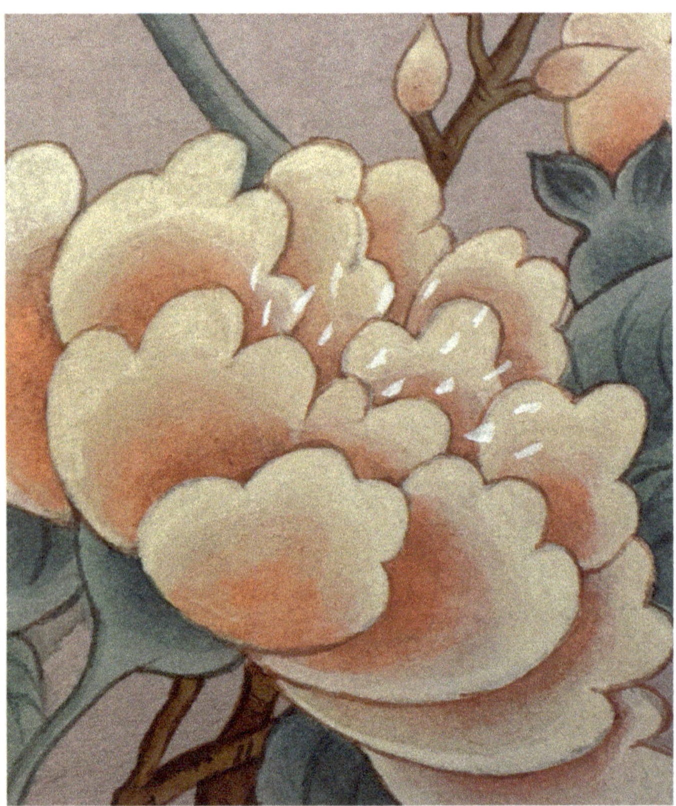

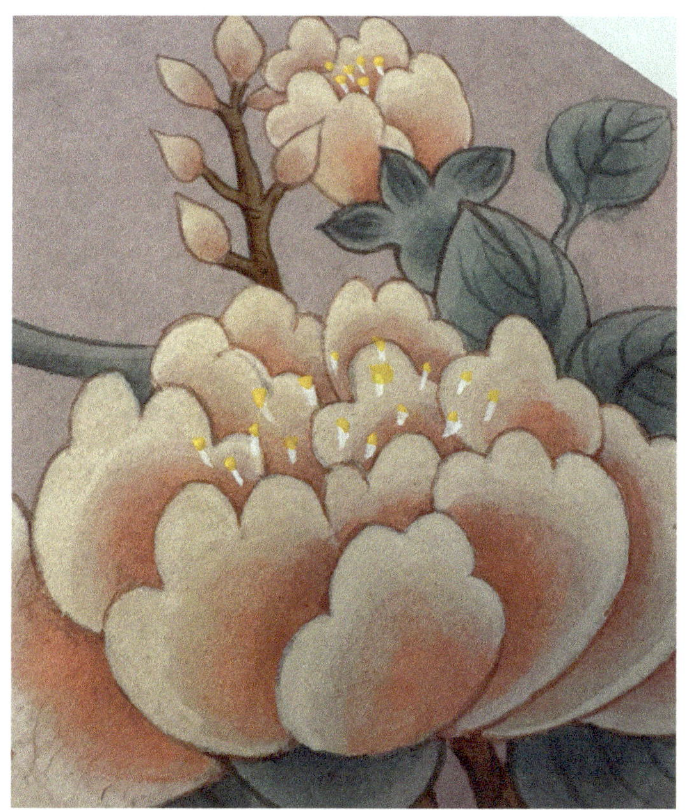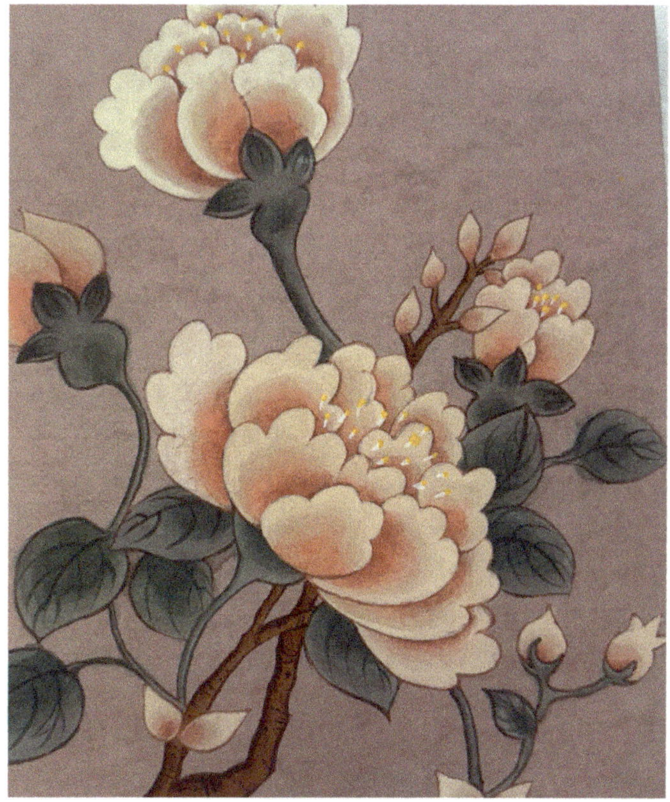

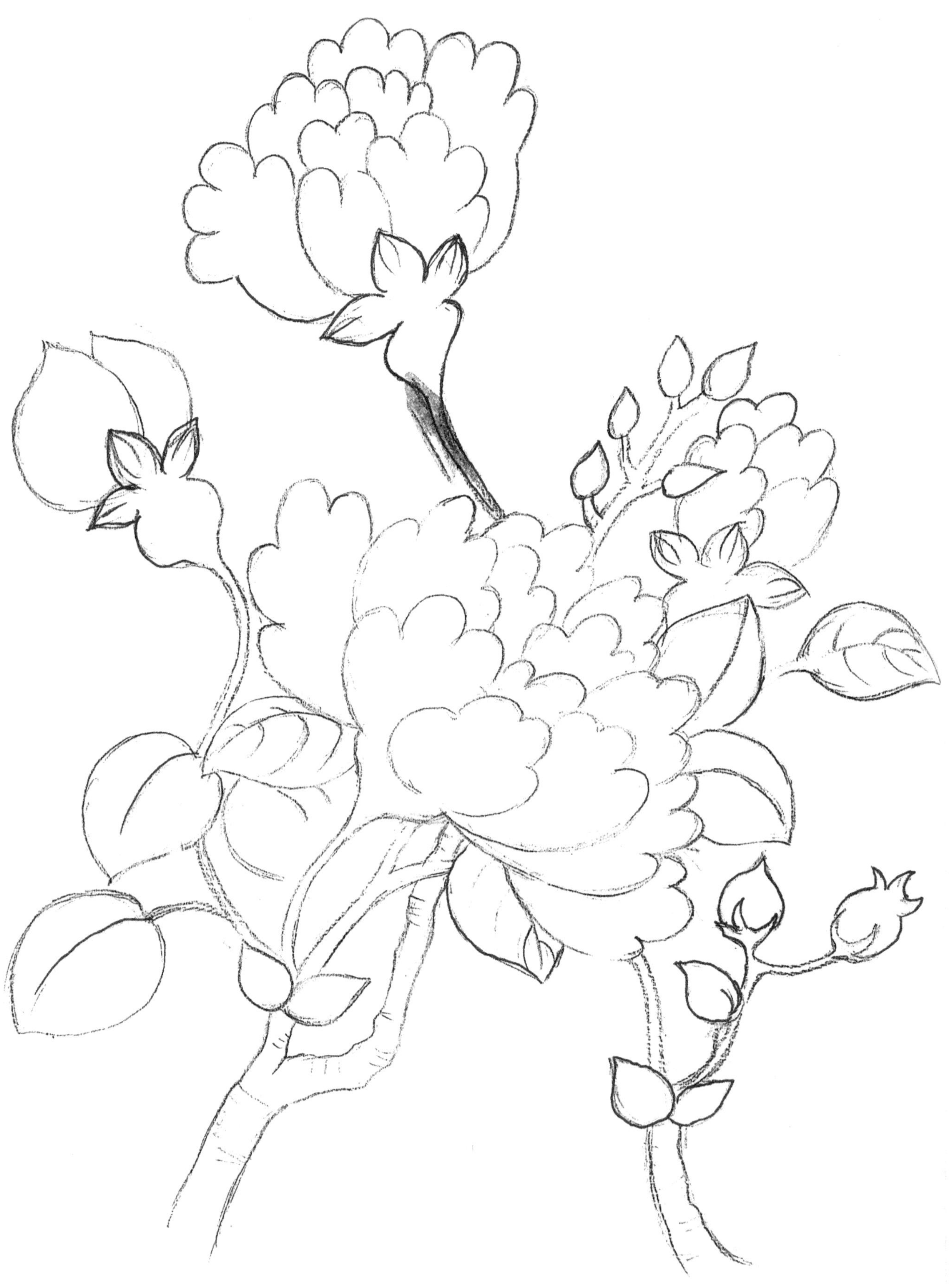

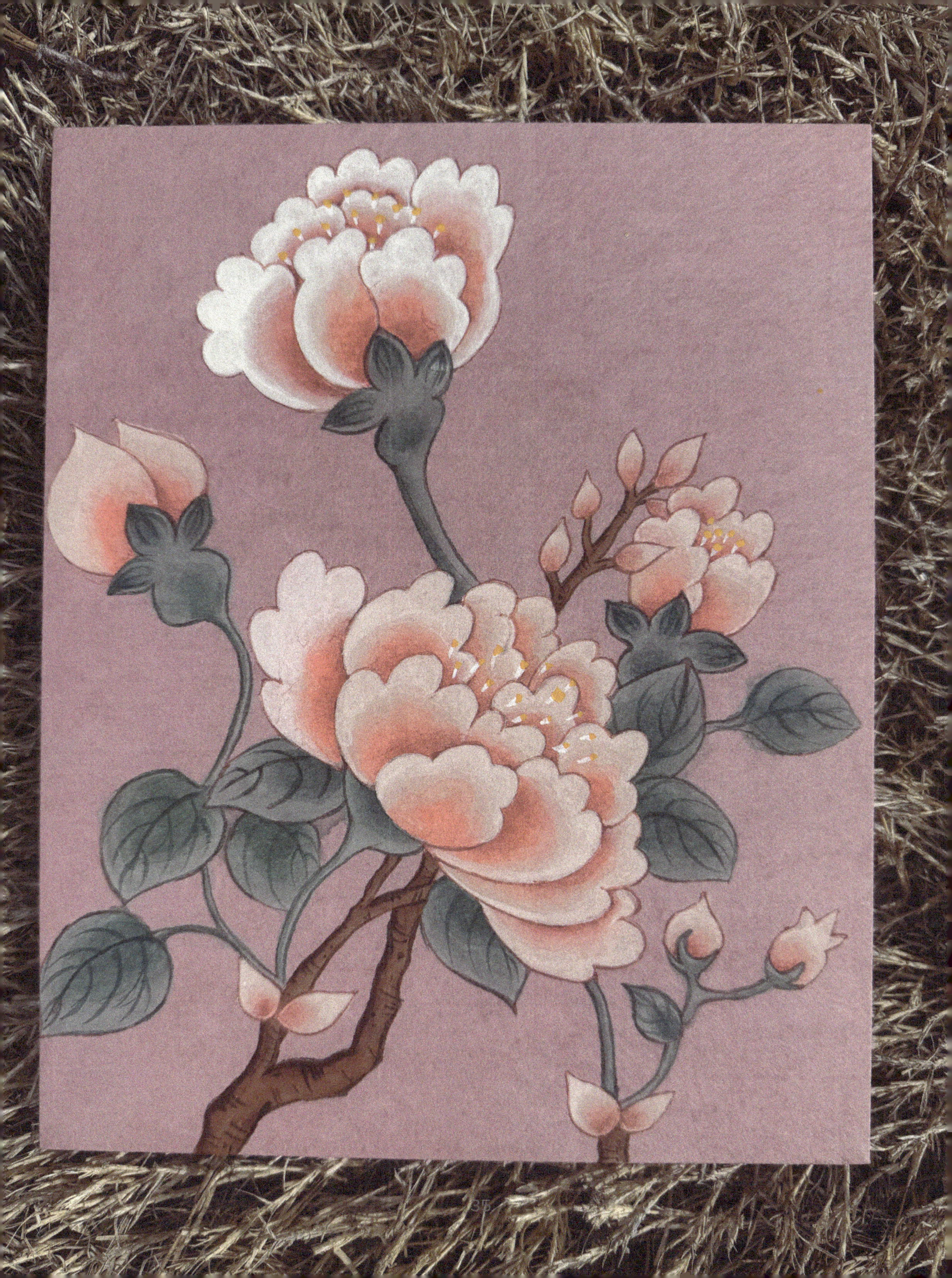

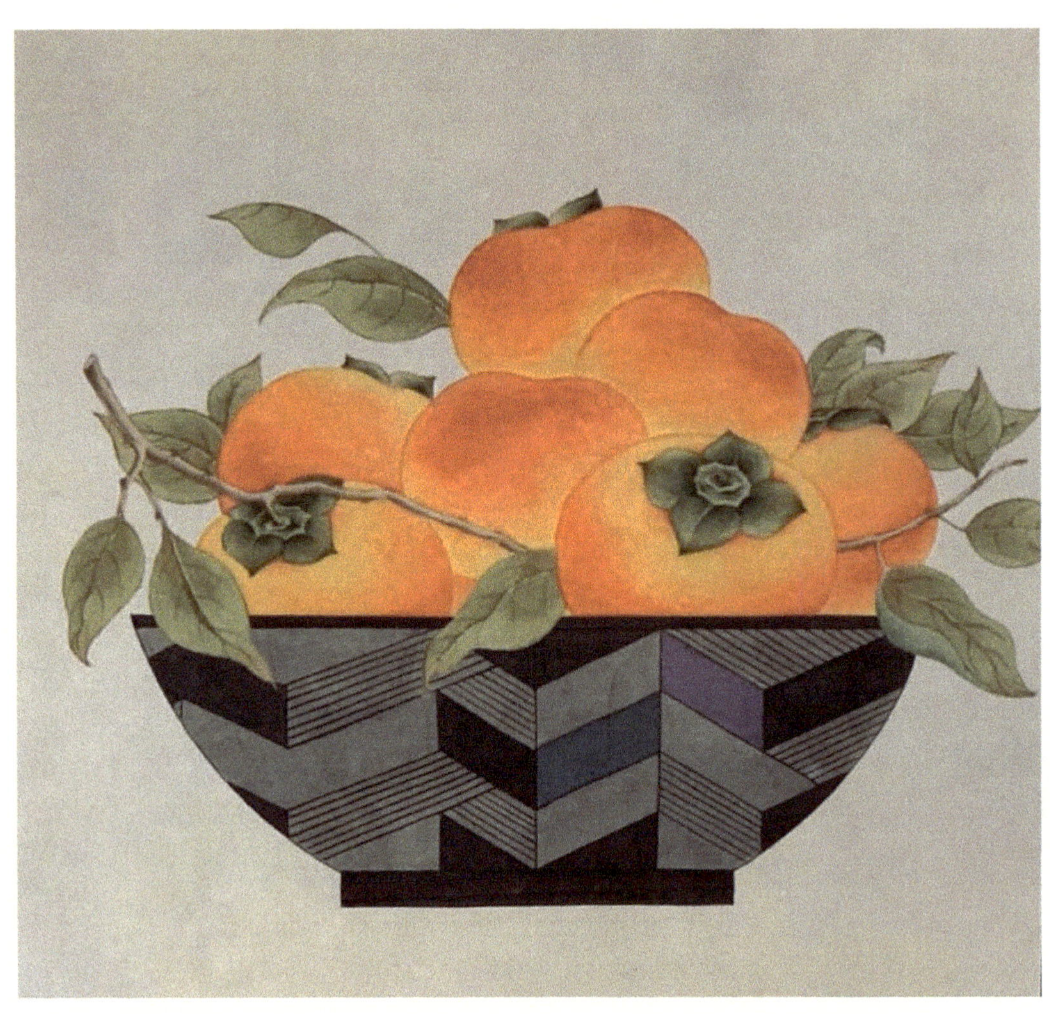

Making Minhwa Today

❀ Minhwa Today ❀

The world has been experiencing a phenomenon known as the Korean Wave, marked by the surge in popularity of Korean music, films, shows, and cuisine. With increasing global attention and success, the talent of Korean artists is being shared and appreciated on a wider scale. I hope this trend fosters greater appreciation and interest in Korean arts, such as minhwa.

In the past decade, minhwa has made a significant comeback in Korea as a popular art form. Numerous art exhibits and workshops are now available, including offerings at universities and private art studios that provide minhwa instruction. What makes minhwa so timeless and popular even after hundreds of years? I can think of a few reasons.

Simple Design

Minhwa designs are characterized by their simple style, making them easily recognizable. Many traditional designs, created by our ancestors hundreds of years ago, are available for public use, allowing artists the freedom to modify or recreate new designs. This flexibility makes it accessible for even beginners to create beautiful minhwa paintings. Originally an art form of the common people, minhwa grew to influence noble art and palatial decorations. Today, it is embraced by modern artists and hobbyists alike.

Symbolism & Practicality

The main subjects of minhwa include nature, animals, and symbols of blessing and luck. These subjects are rich in symbolism related to hope and prayers. For instance, blooming flowers represent wealth and prosperity, lovebirds signify love and peace for couples and families, while insects and fruits symbolize fertility and growth. Tigers and dragons are often depicted for protection and blessings. Historically, displaying these artworks was believed to attract positive energies and blessings, making minhwa popular for home decoration as well as for rituals and celebrations. In modern times, minhwa continues to influence fashion, home décor, and the illustration industry.

Minhwa & Digital Arts

Among younger generations, digitally created minhwa is gaining popularity. Artists are leveraging advanced digital illustration technologies to produce minhwa that is more detailed, three-dimensional, or even animated, showcasing the innovative spirit of modern digital artists.

Happy Marriage of Old & New

Many artists continue to embrace and preserve traditional minhwa styles, much like our ancestors did. At the same time, numerous contemporary artists are reinterpreting minhwa through modern perspectives. Some are incorporating the traditional Korean color palette of the Five Elements (Oheng) (blue, yellow, red, white, and black) into various mediums and new styles. There's a growing trend of exploring modern themes and subjects, such as equality and justice, within minhwa.

Minhwa is not simply an ancient painting style; it is a unique artistic genre that embodies the spirit and character of the Korean people. It serves as an important bridge between the ancient and modern worlds, continuing to promote the beauty and wisdom of our ancestral arts to the rest of the world.

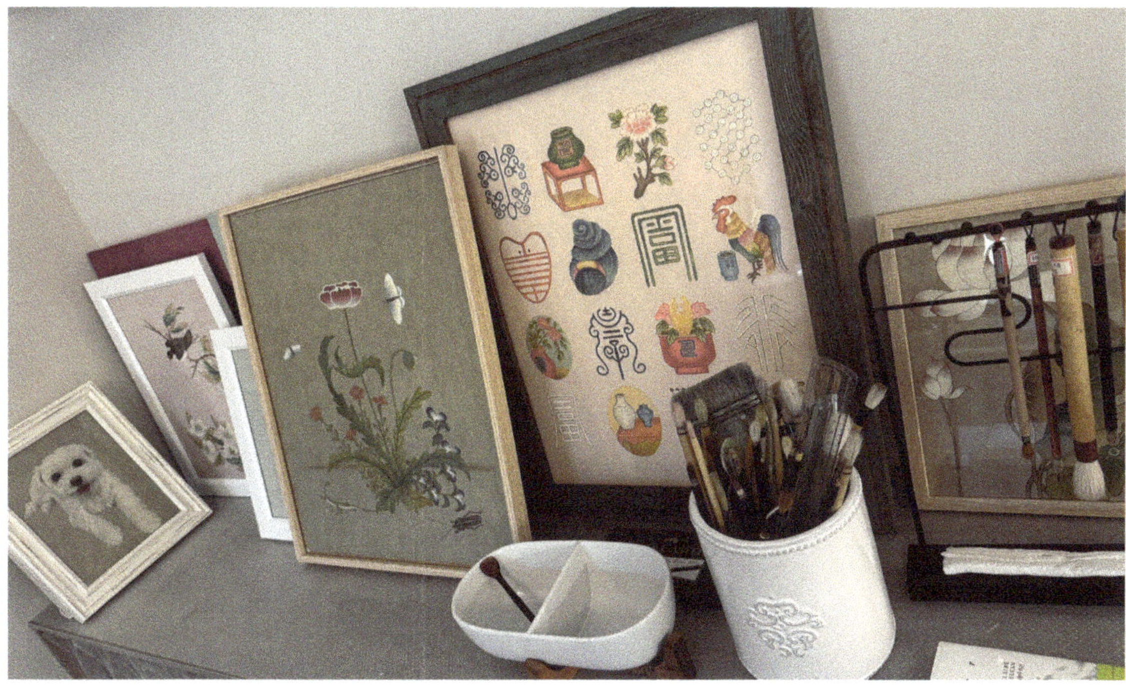

Using Different Mediums for Minhwa

One of the biggest challenges for minhwa artists in the West today is the difficulty in obtaining the necessary materials for traditional Eastern Fine Arts. It's ironic that this folk art form, which originated with everyday people, now requires specialized supplies.

When artists cannot find the specific paints made for Eastern Fine Arts, they can use art supplies such as watercolors or gouache instead. Additionally, while hanji paper is traditionally used, regular watercolor paper can also serve as a suitable alternative.

For example, one of my middle school students used watercolor paints and conventional art paper to create an intricate traditional minhwa design. It took him three months to complete, and the final result looks fantastic!

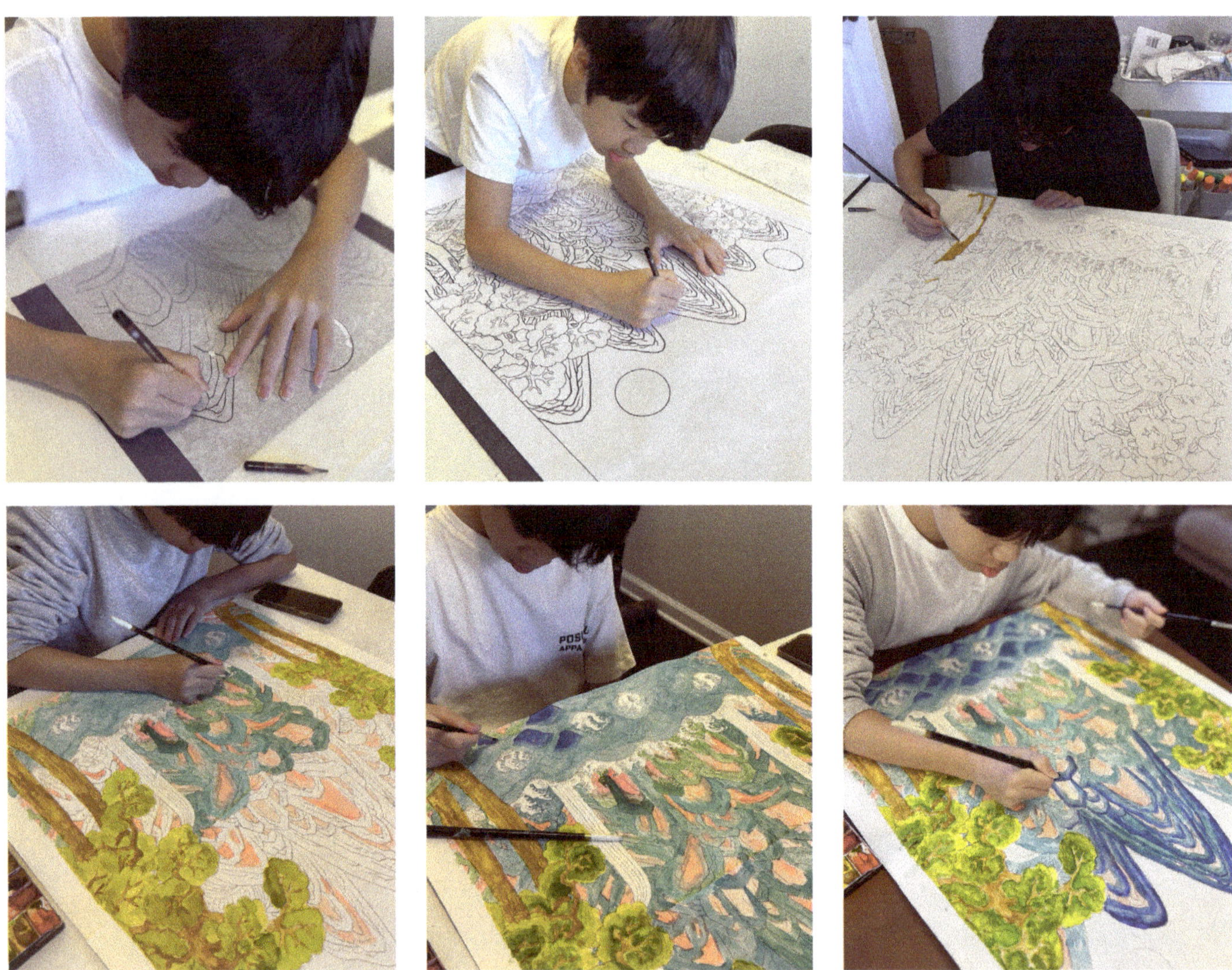

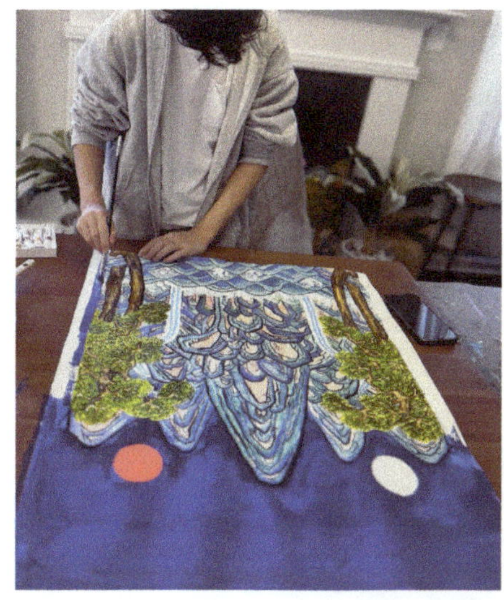
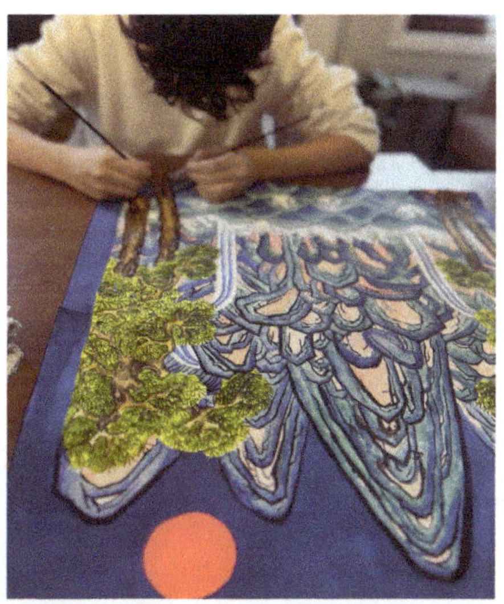
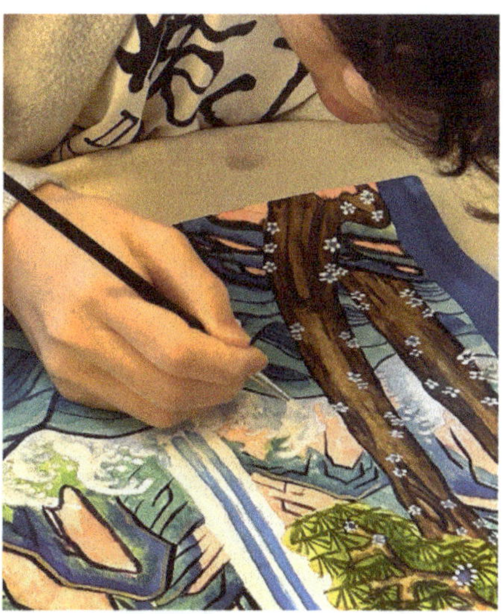
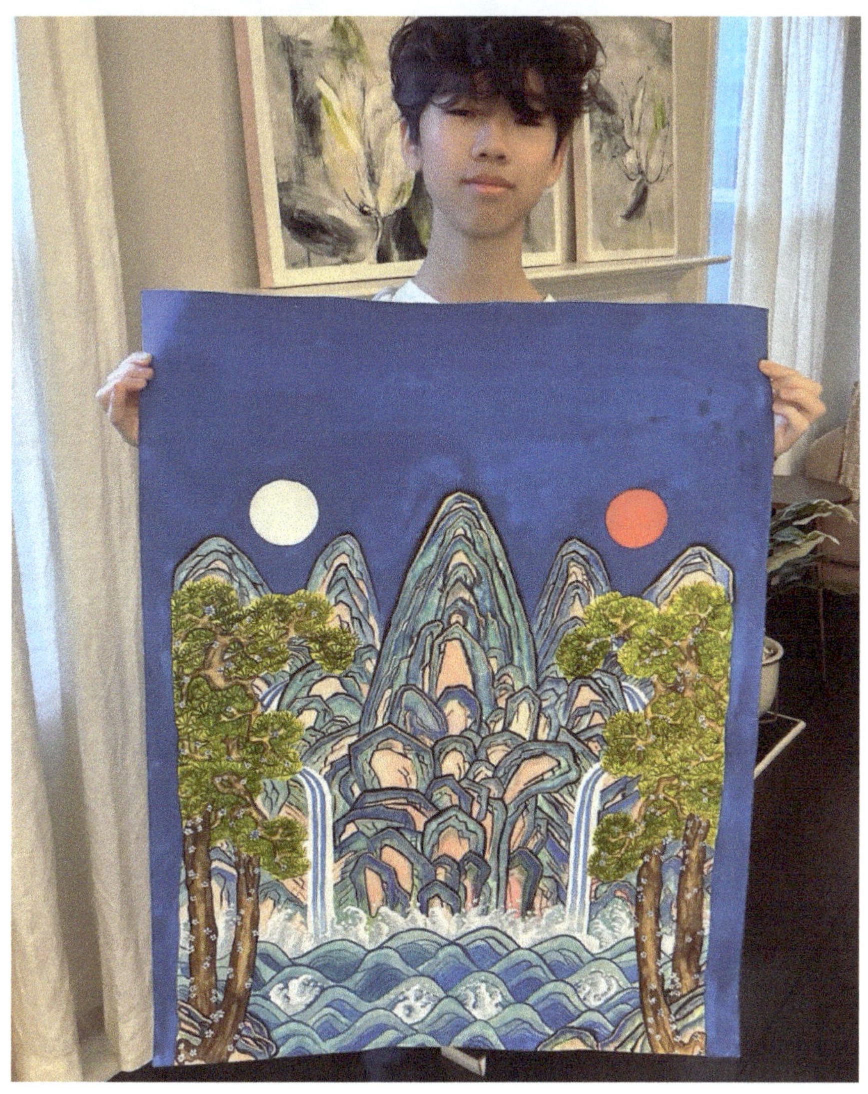

Pets as Minhwa Subjects

One of my favorite modern trends in minhwa is using our pets as models. During the time when traditional minhwa flourished, our ancestors did not have the same special relationships with their pets as we do today. Nowadays, pets are considered part of our families and everyday life. What a wonderful way to honor and appreciate our furry companions while wishing for their long, healthy lives and blessings for the entire family!

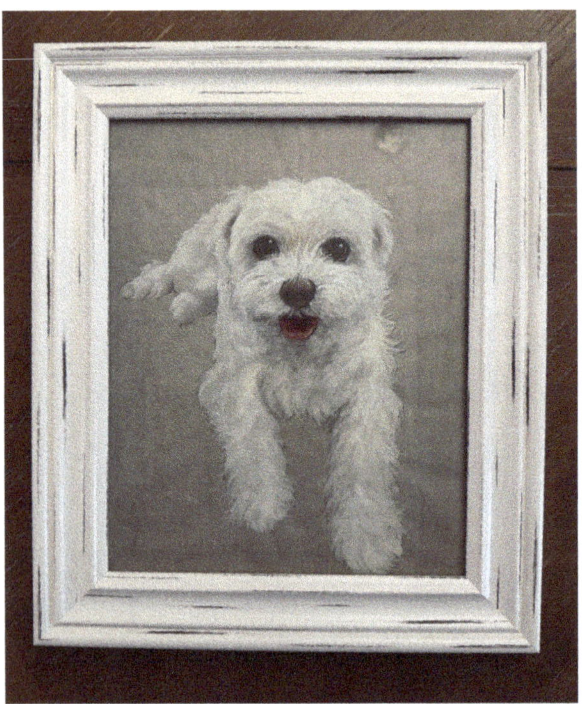 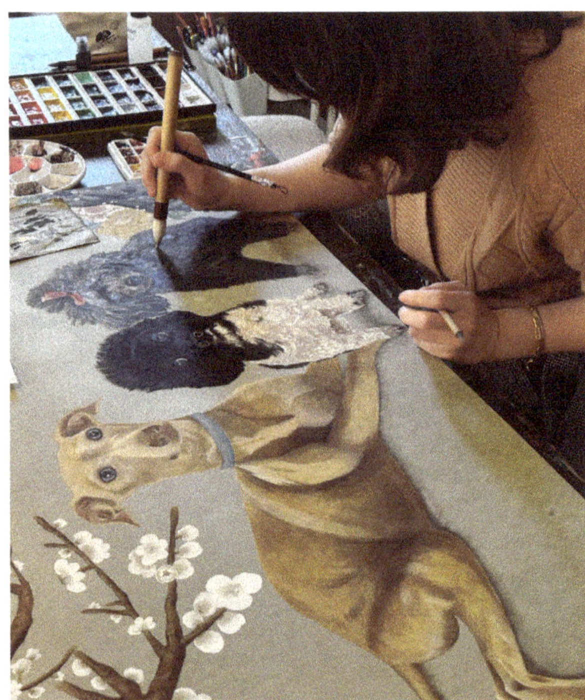

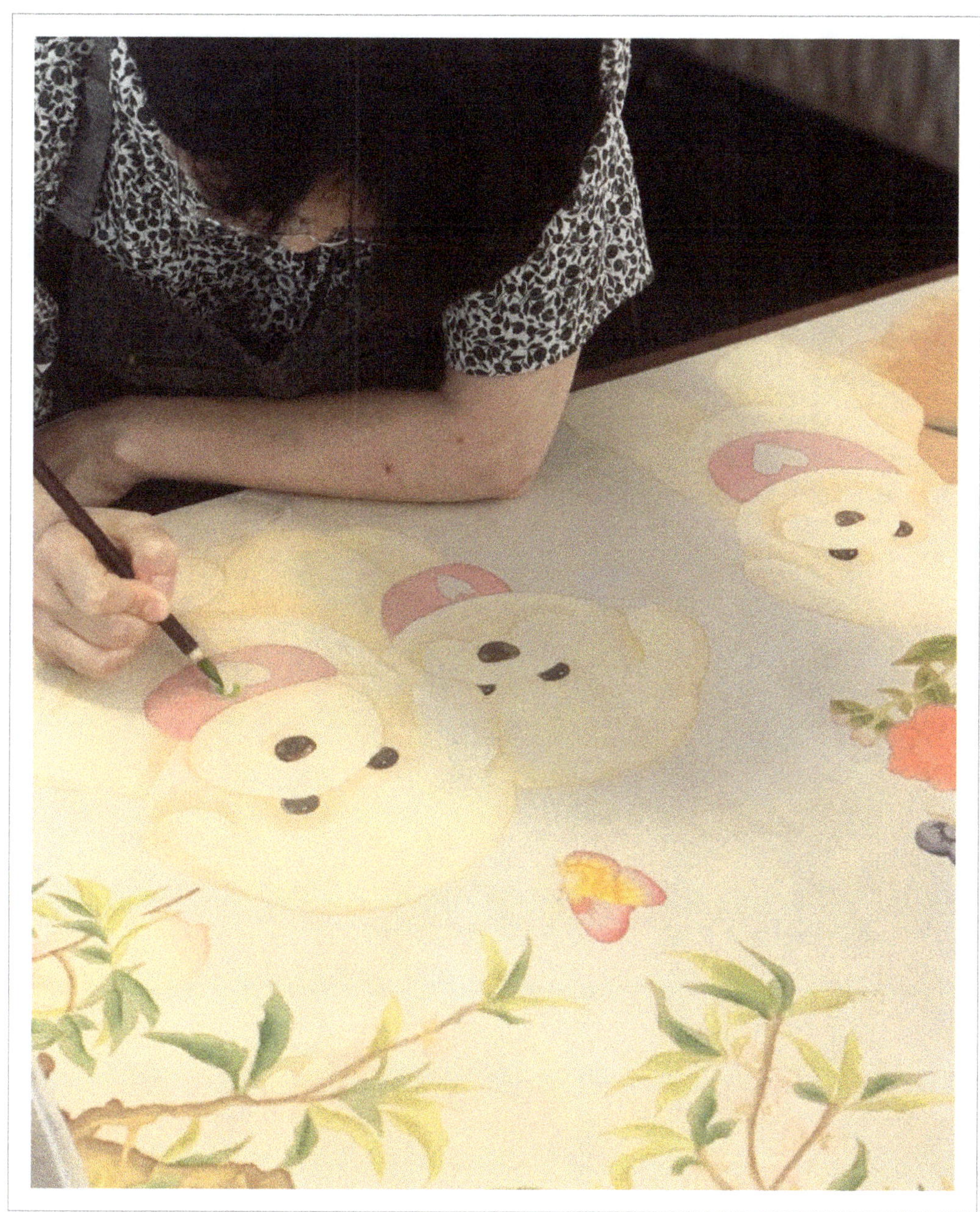

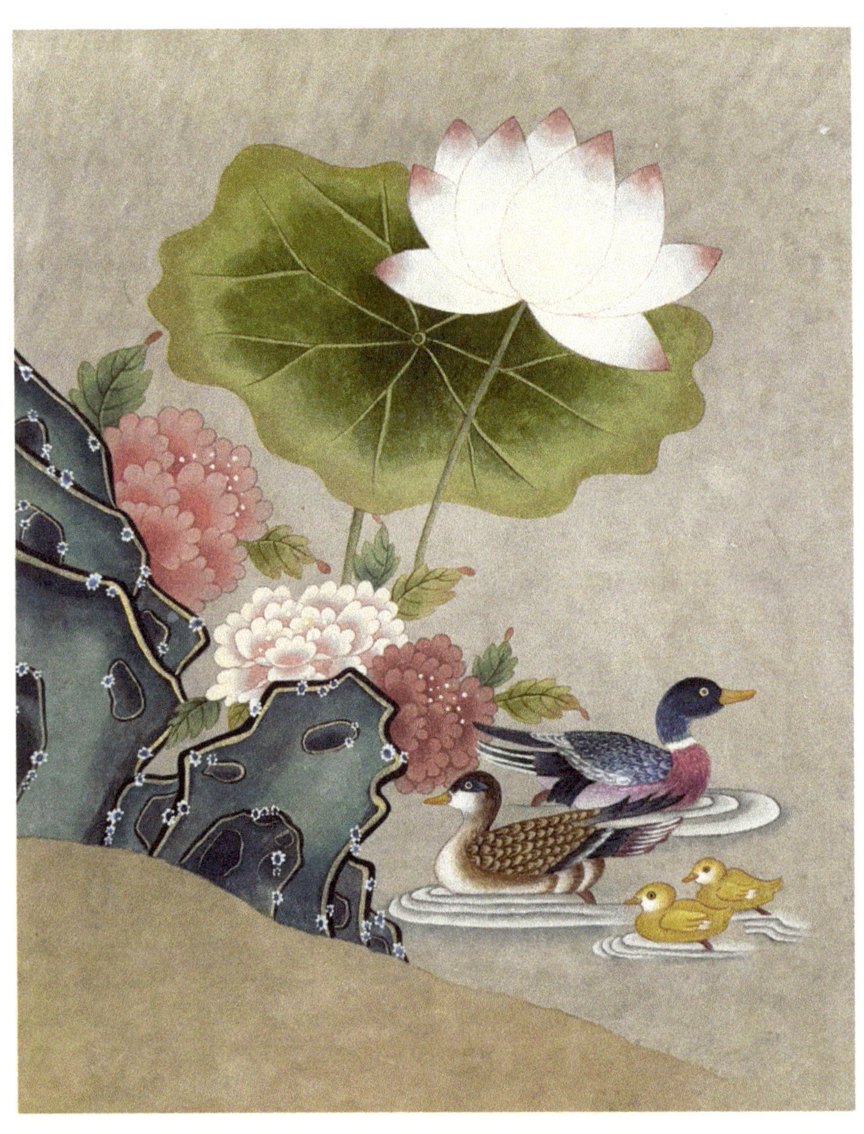

Practice Arts

Popular Minhwa Symbolism

Peonies - Considered the most ornate flowers in Korea, peonies represent prosperity and wealth.

Royal (Ornate) Peonies - Symbolizing full blooms of life, paintings of fancy peonies represent prosperity and wealth for the entire family, including all descendants. Such images of royal peonies had been used to create decorative folding screens for women's quarters or special occasions, such as weddings and other celebrations.

Lotus Flower - Symbolizing "grace under pressure," the lotus represents purity, integrity, and honesty.

Tiger & Magpie - Tigers are guardians and protectors against bad spirits. Magpies are messengers of good news. Painted together, they represent wishes for protection and blessing.

Fruit Bowls - Symbolizing a vessel holding the results of fruition, these images represent abundance, prosperity, fertility, and healthy births.

Banana Tree Leaves - By painting dying leaves and new leaves together, the art symbolizes resilience, rising above challenges, and tenacity.

Plant & Insects - Symbolizing their natural vitality through the life cycles, plants and insects are painted together to symbolize resilience, vitality, and health, especially for the elderly.

Flowers & Birds - Images of lovebirds or a family of birds with flowers represent wishes for a long, healthy, and happy marriage and family life.

Flowers & Butterflies - Images of butterflies and flowers represent love, romance, and a happy marriage.

Fish Turning to Dragon - Depicting a transformation from a mere fish to the powerful dragon, the image represents wishes for the descendants' success, fortune, fame, and luck.

Blessing Letter - By decorating the letter itself or around the letter, these arts represent prayers for the meaning of the letter (blessing).

Books & Things - The love of books by King Jeongjo of the Joseon dynasty sparked a trend where paintings of books combined with other everyday items became a popular minhwa subject. They tend to be more focused on decorative and creative images, rather than realistic images.

Sun, Moon, and Five Peaks - Originally used only as a backdrop in the emperor's quarters of the Joseon kingdom, the image became a popular minhwa subject for modern artists. The sun and moon are risen together in the sky above the five mountain peaks with other natural elements of the Korean land—ocean waves, rocks, and pine trees.

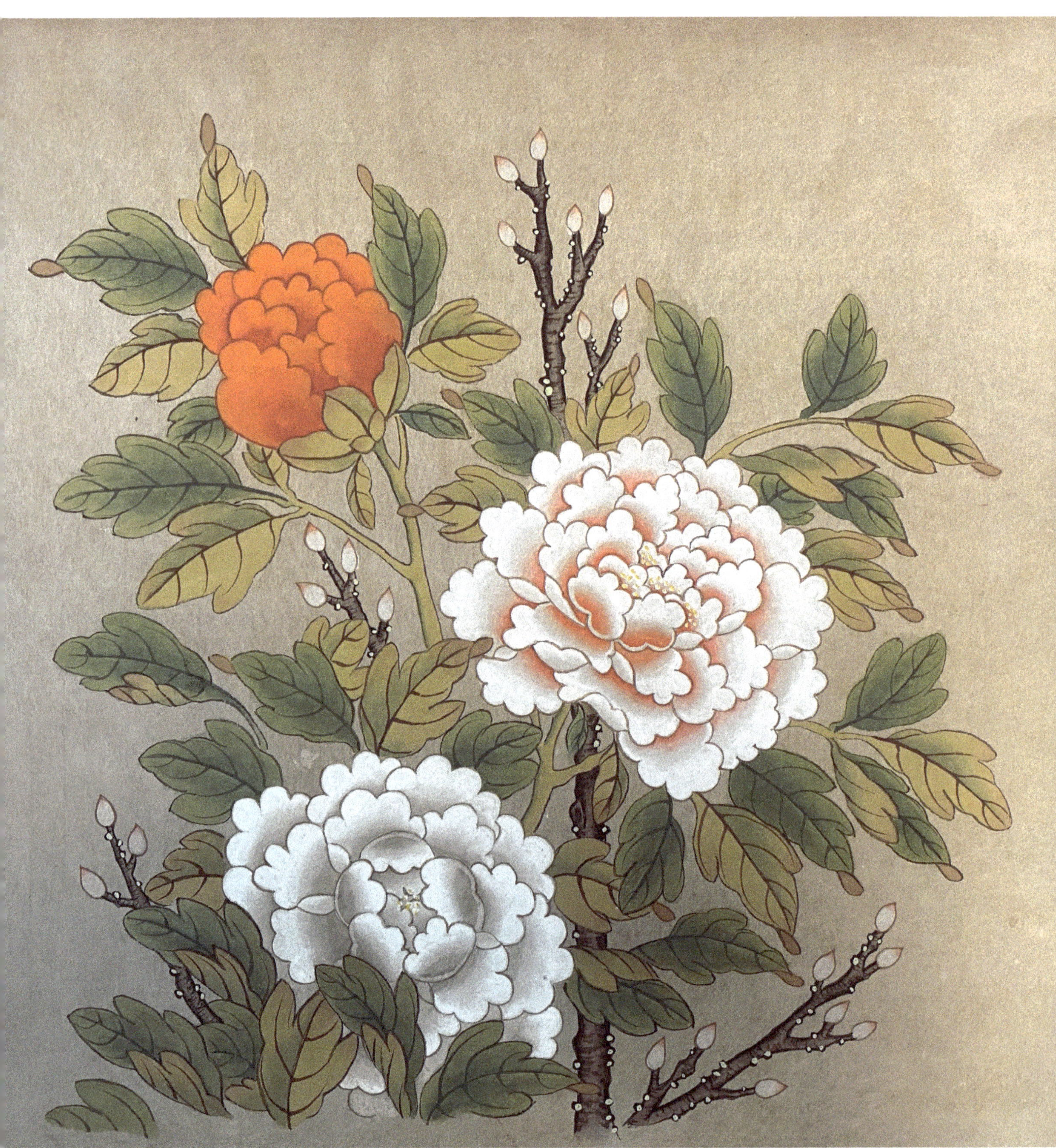

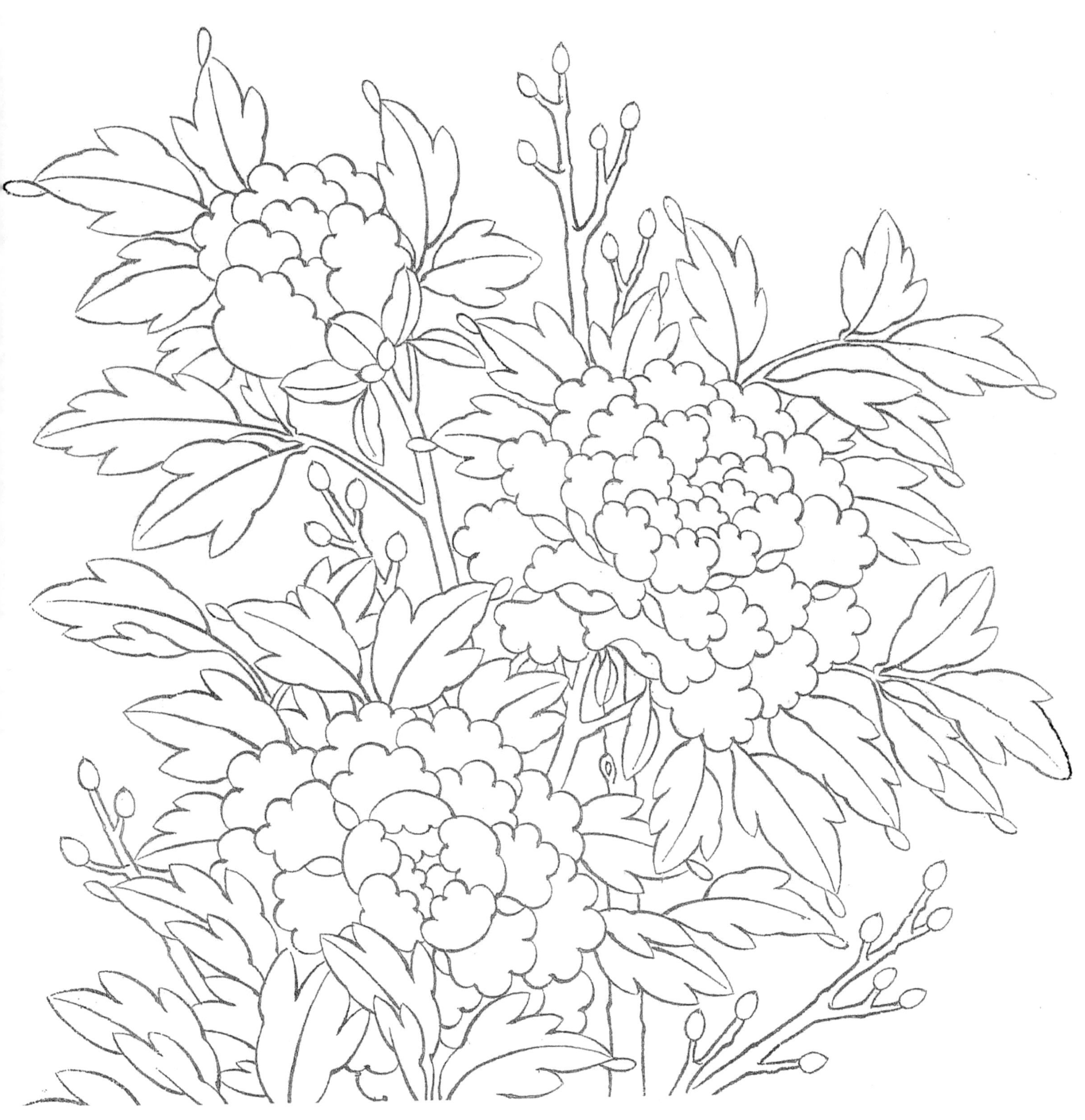

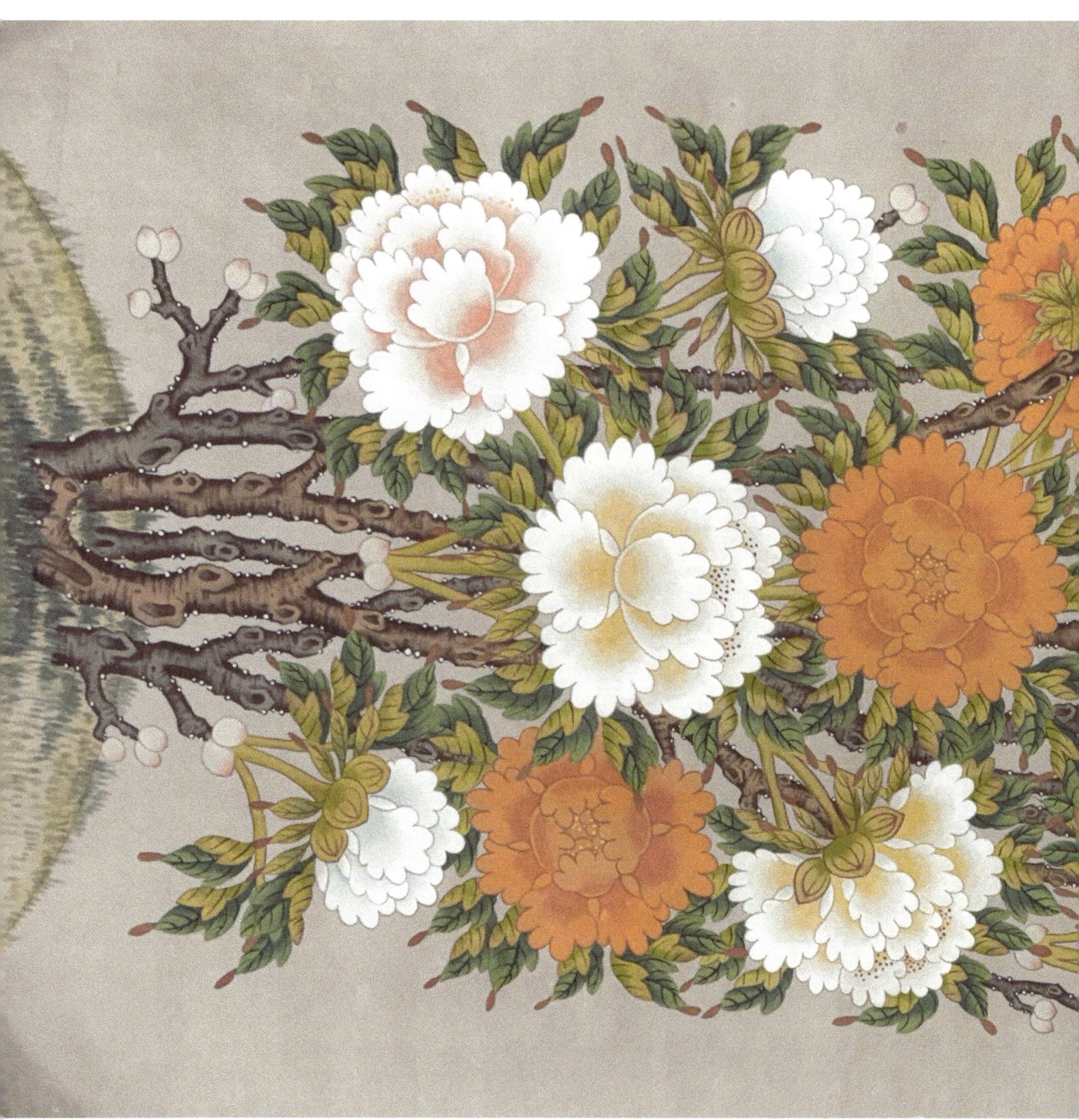

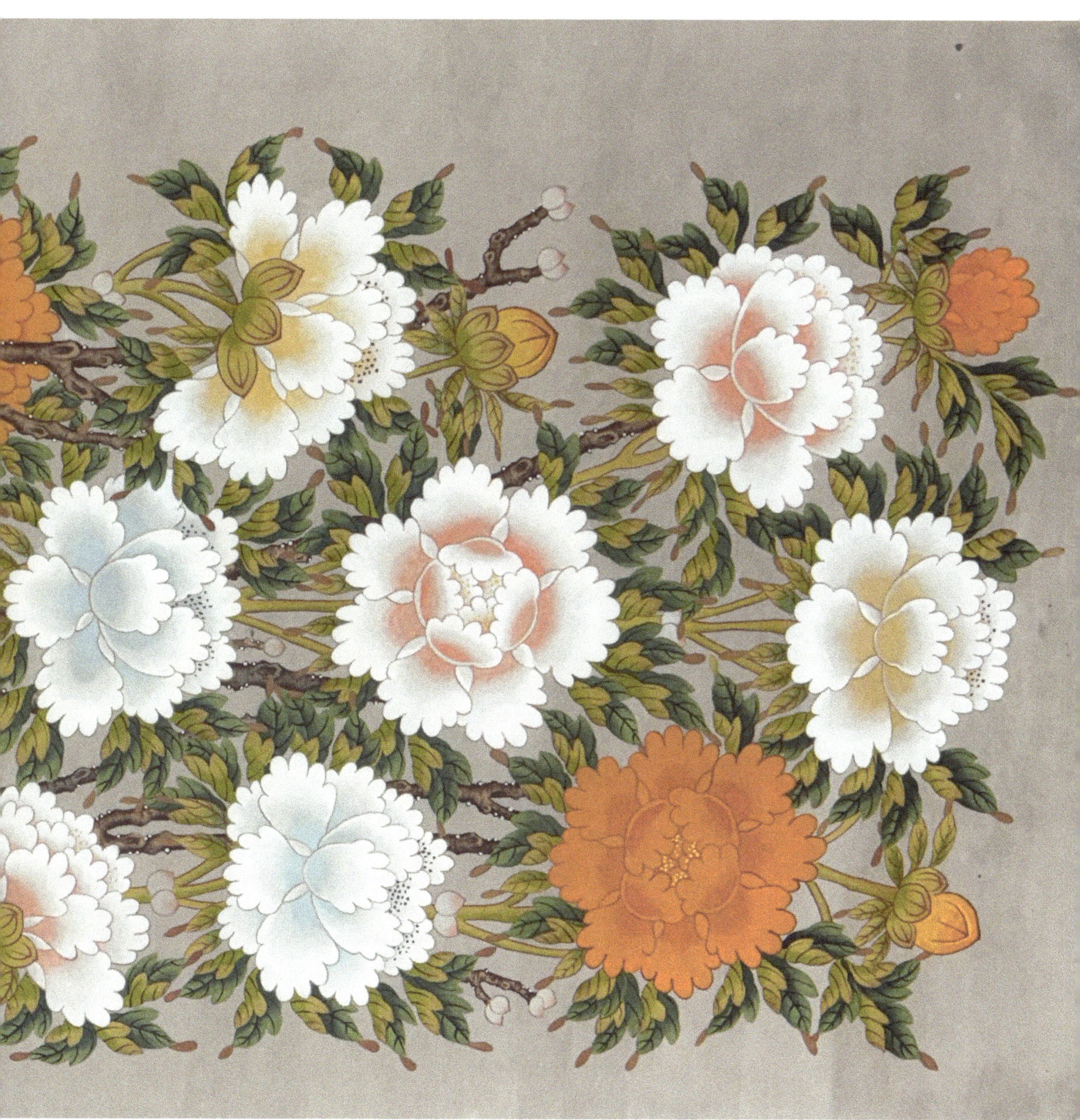

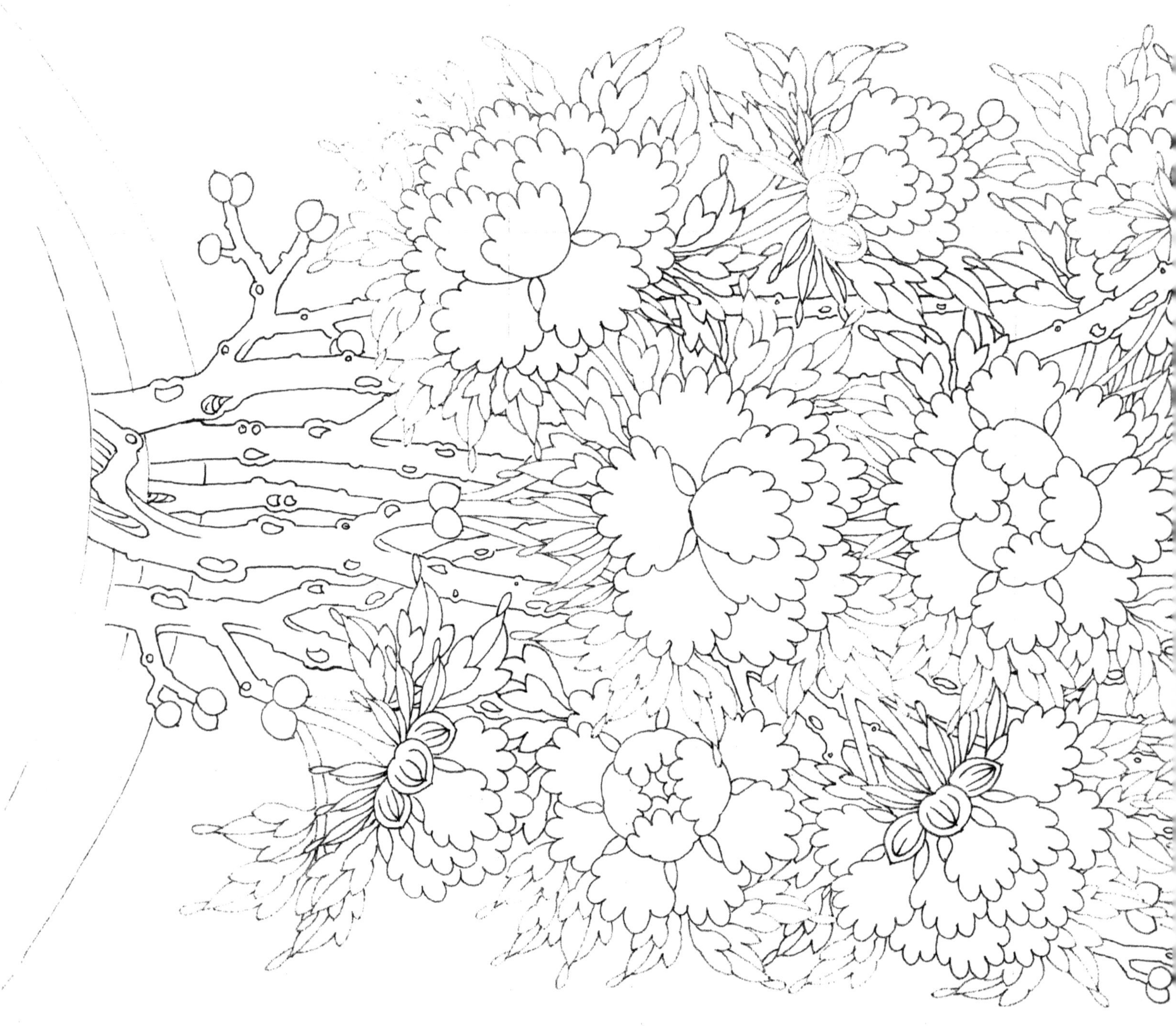

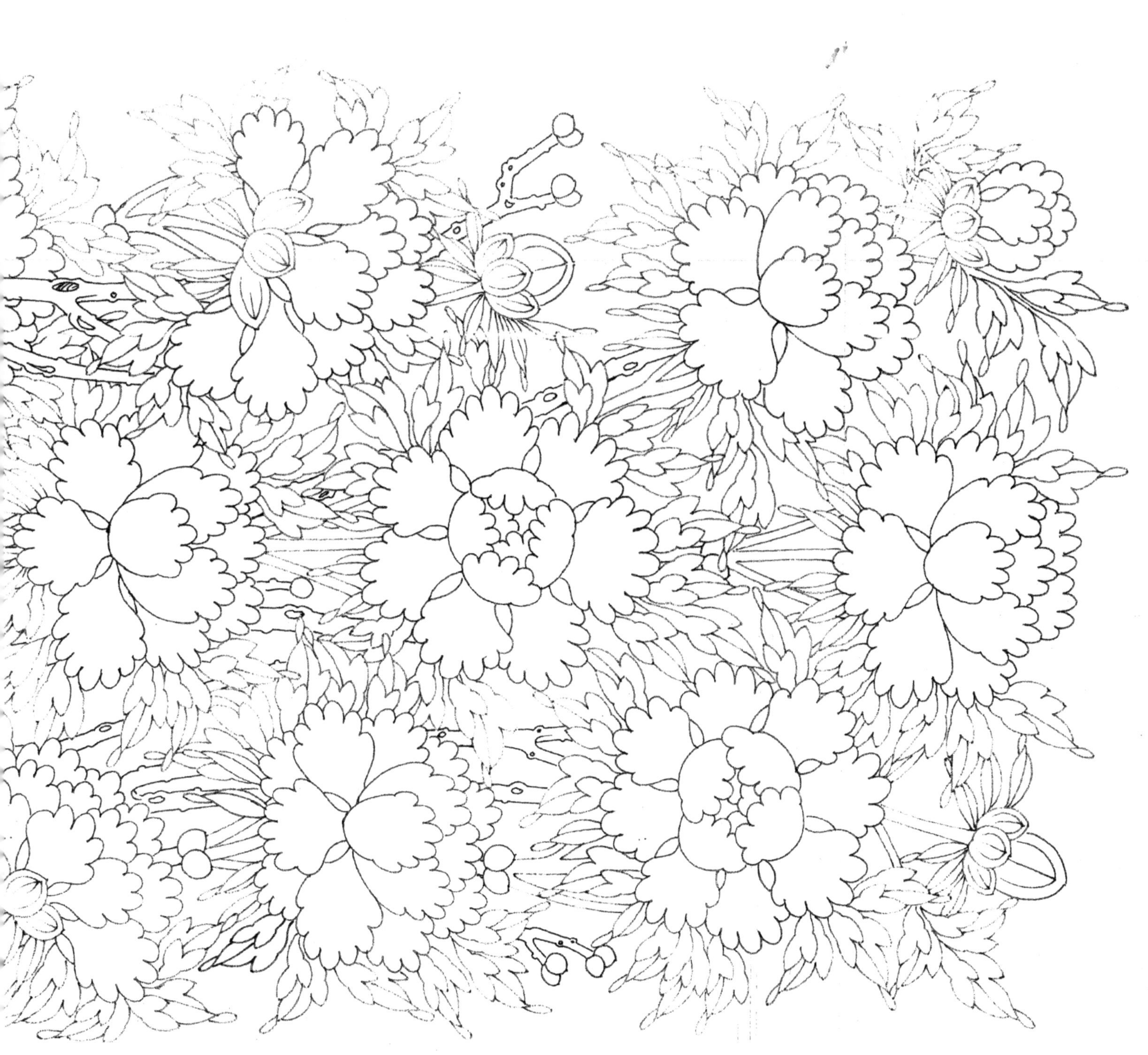

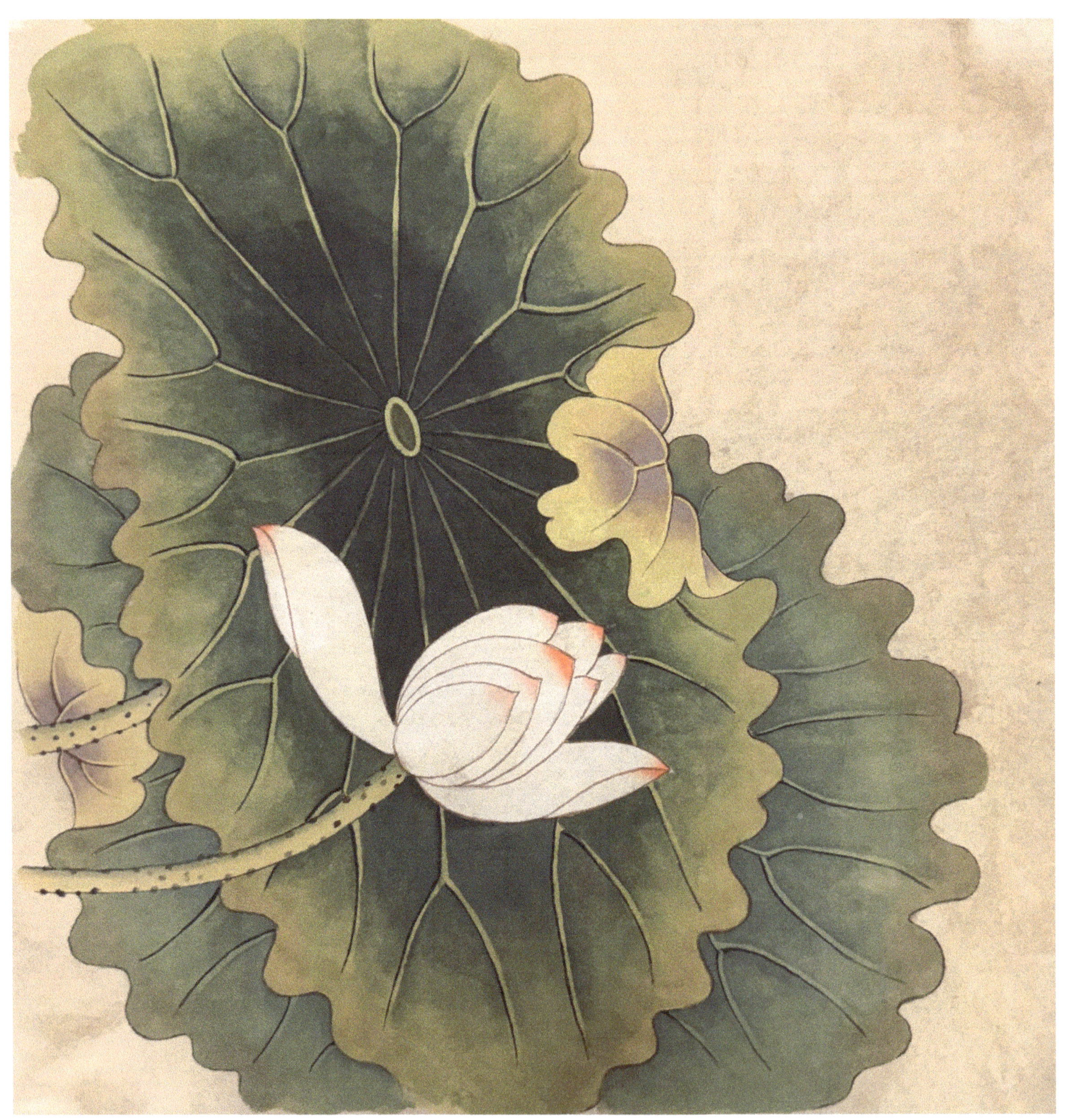

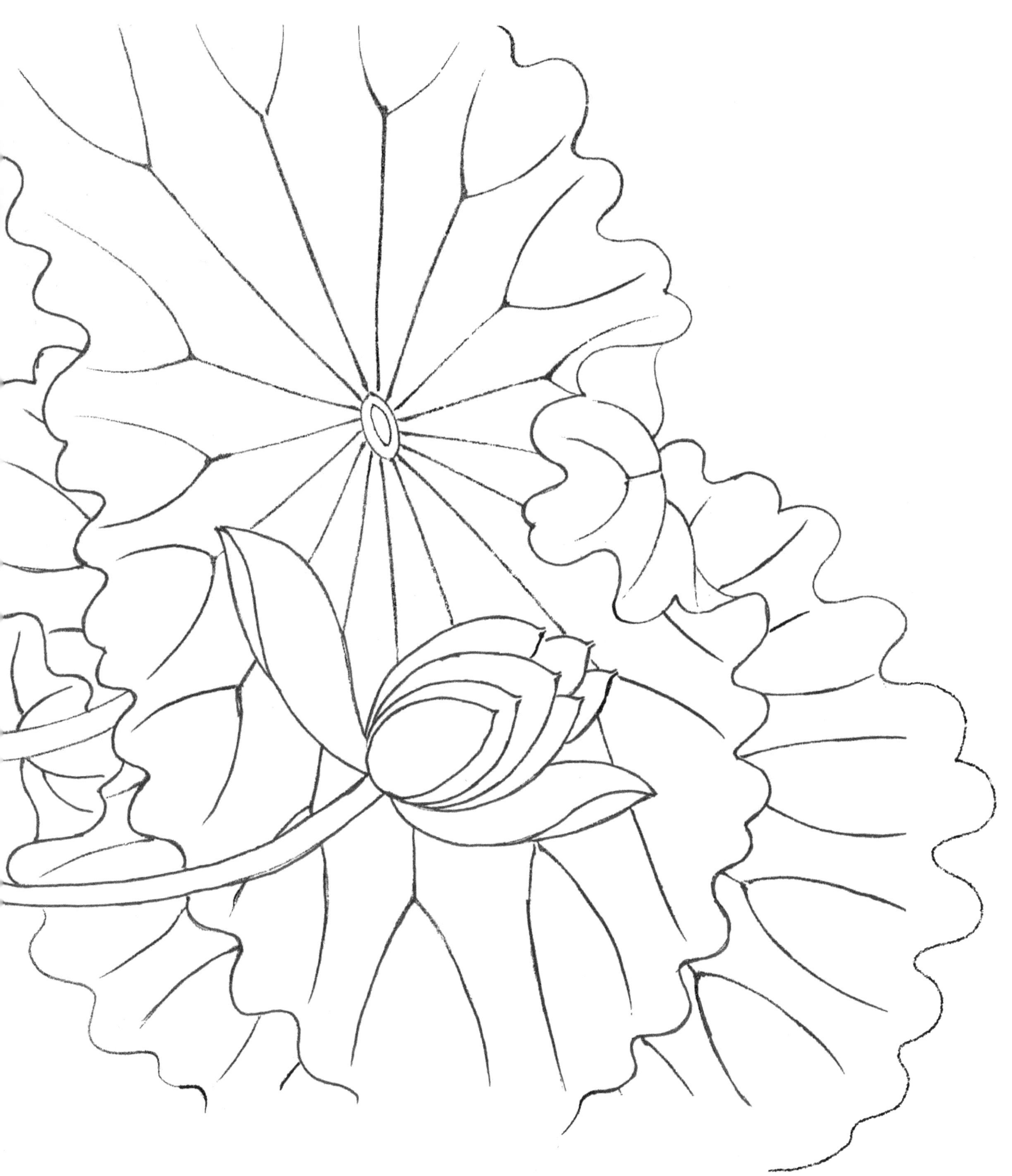

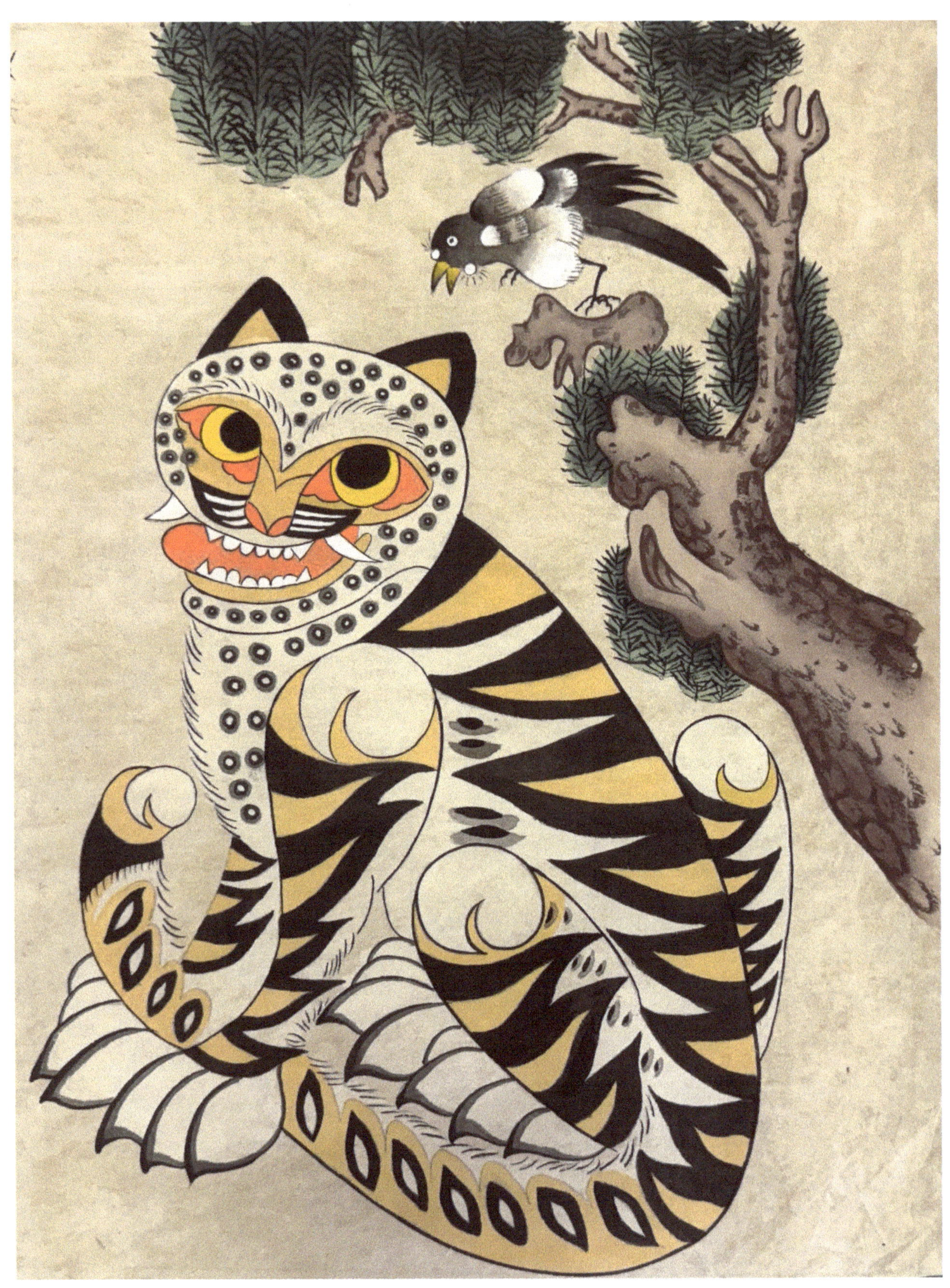

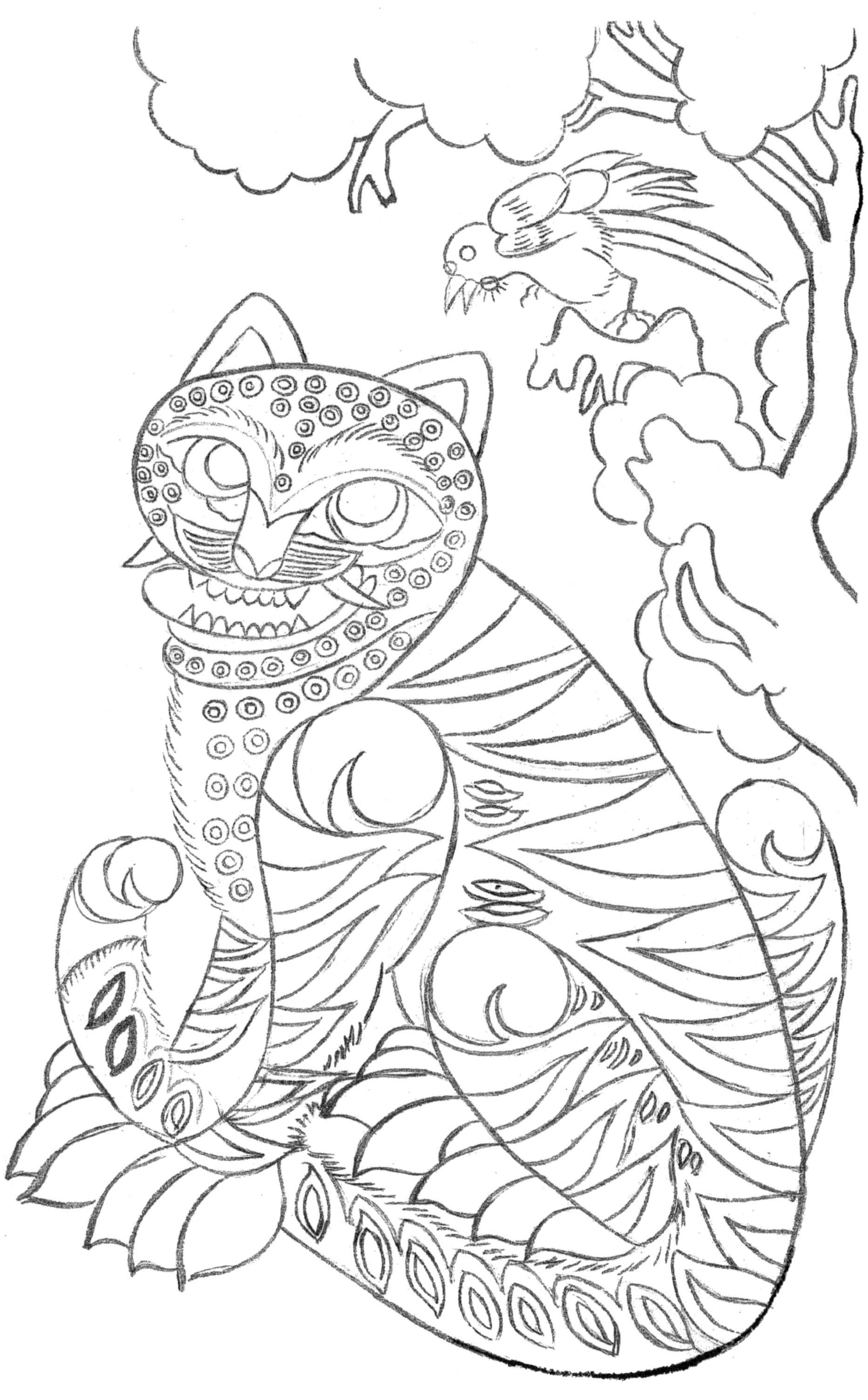

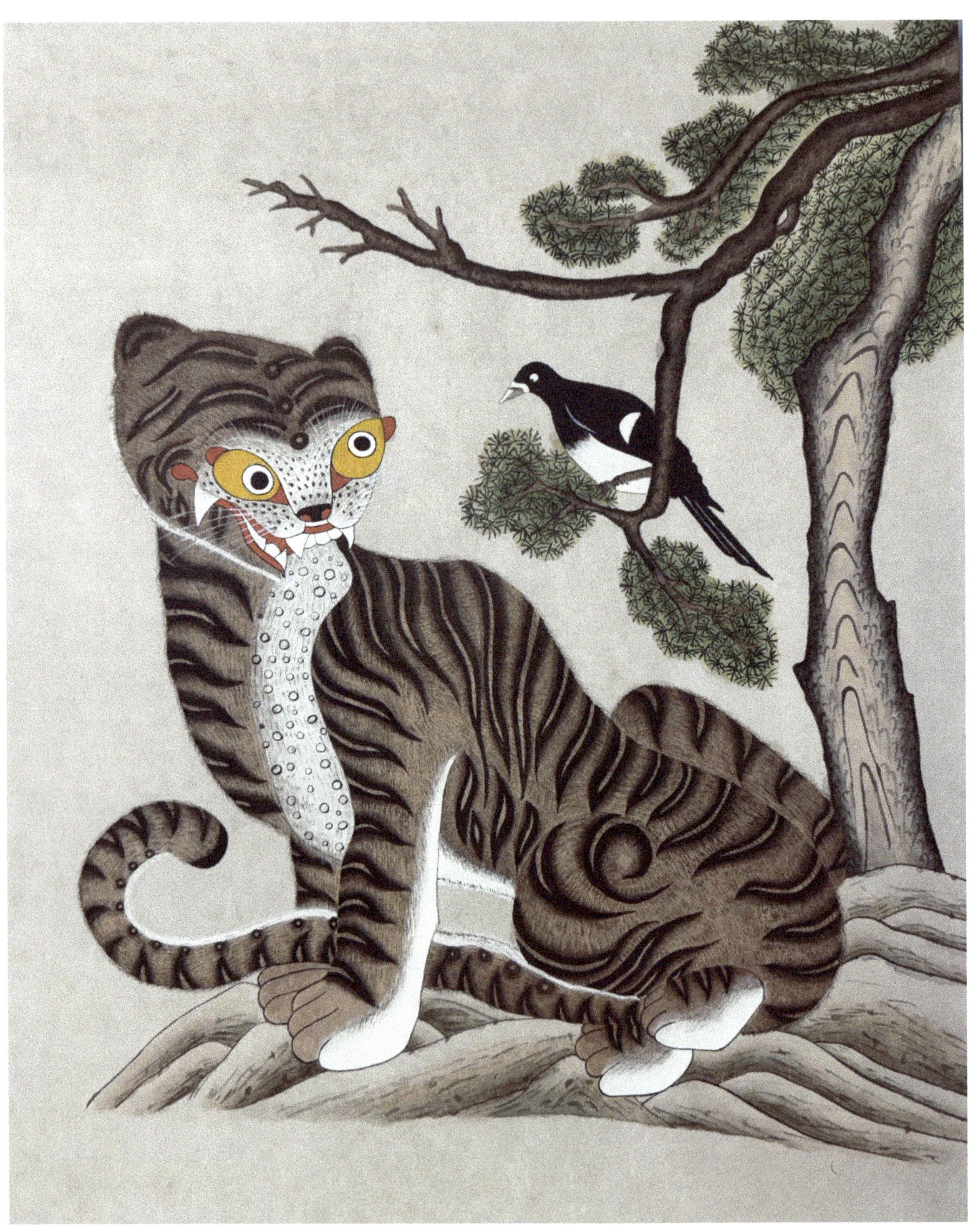

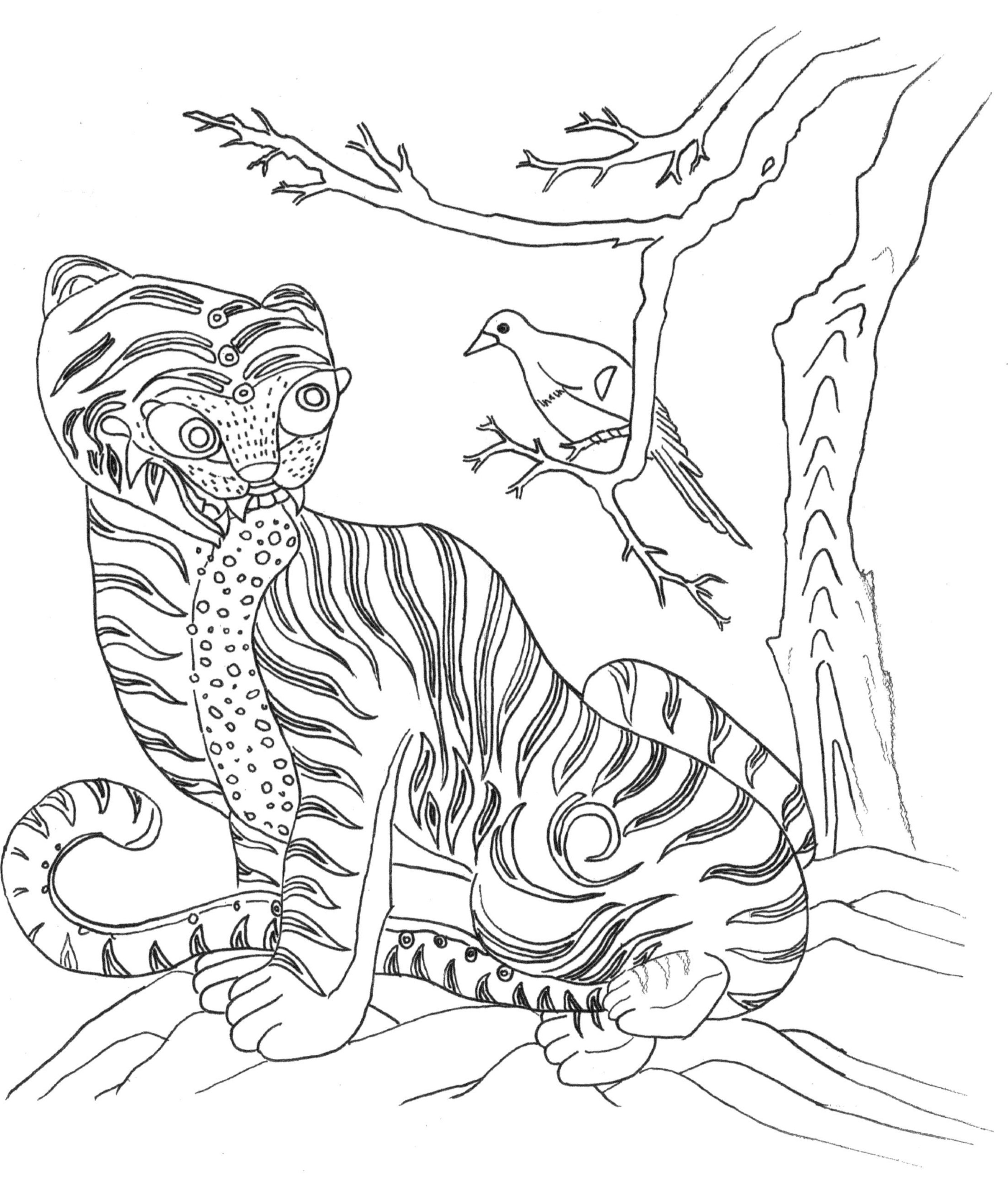

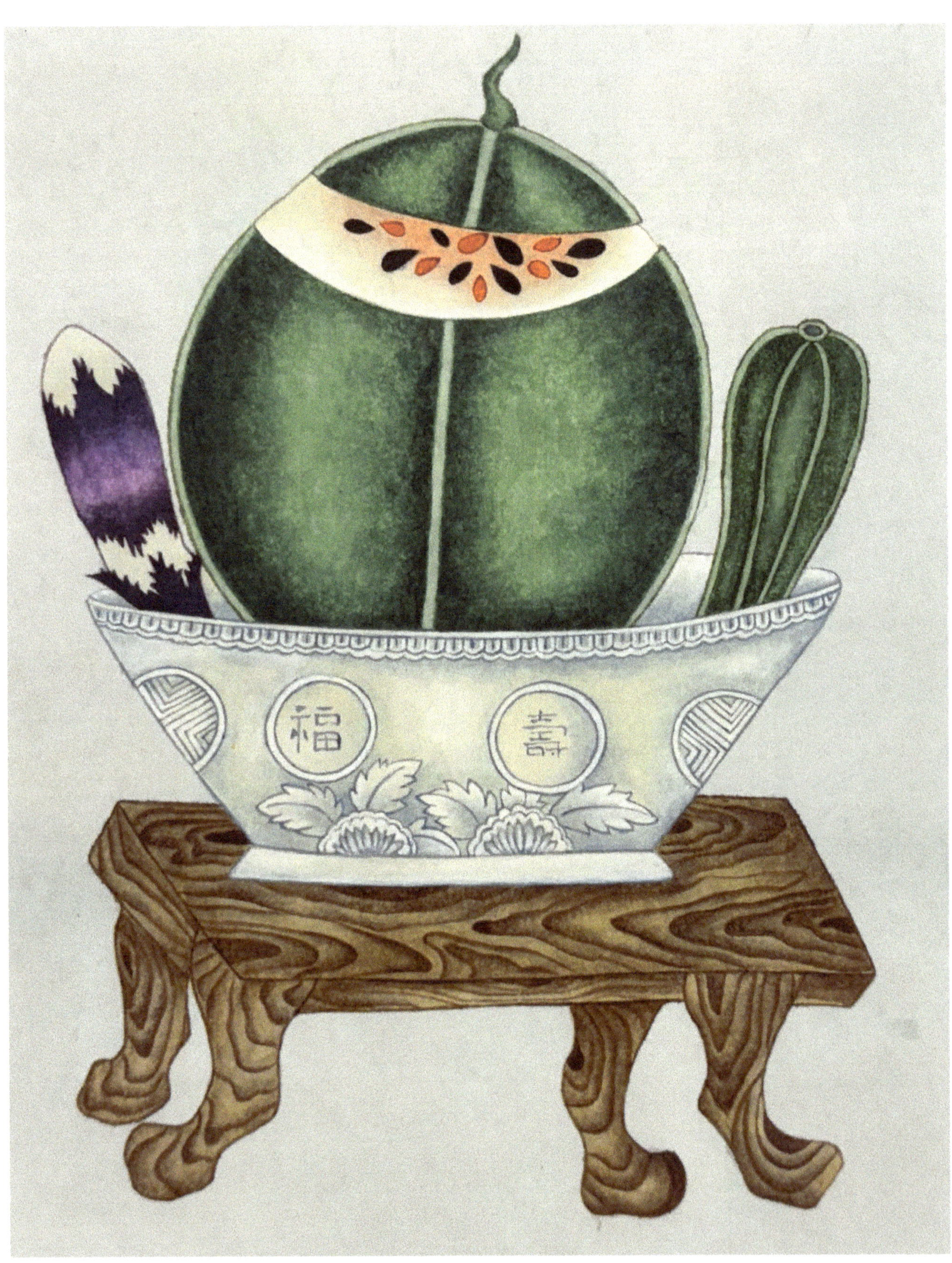

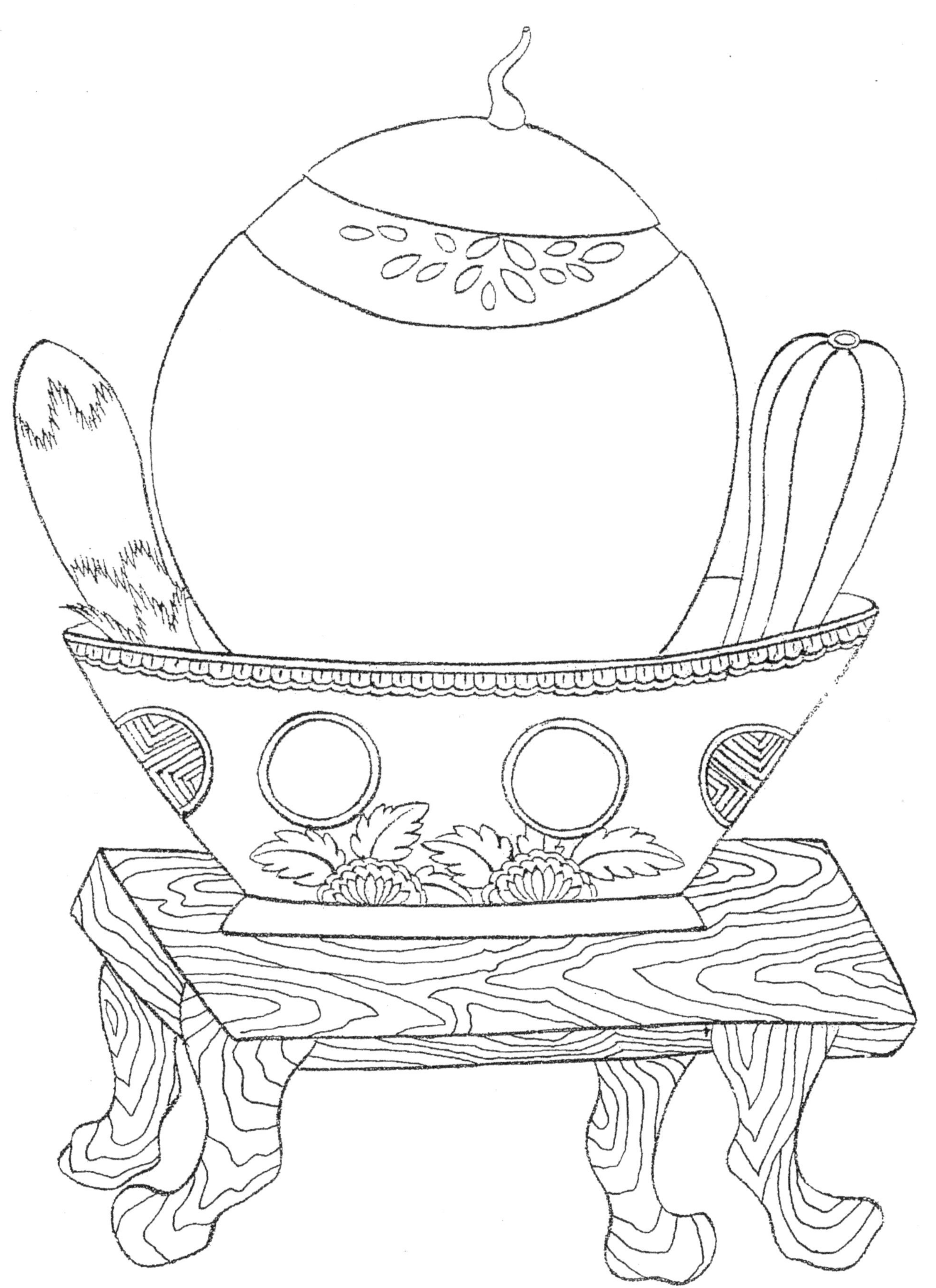

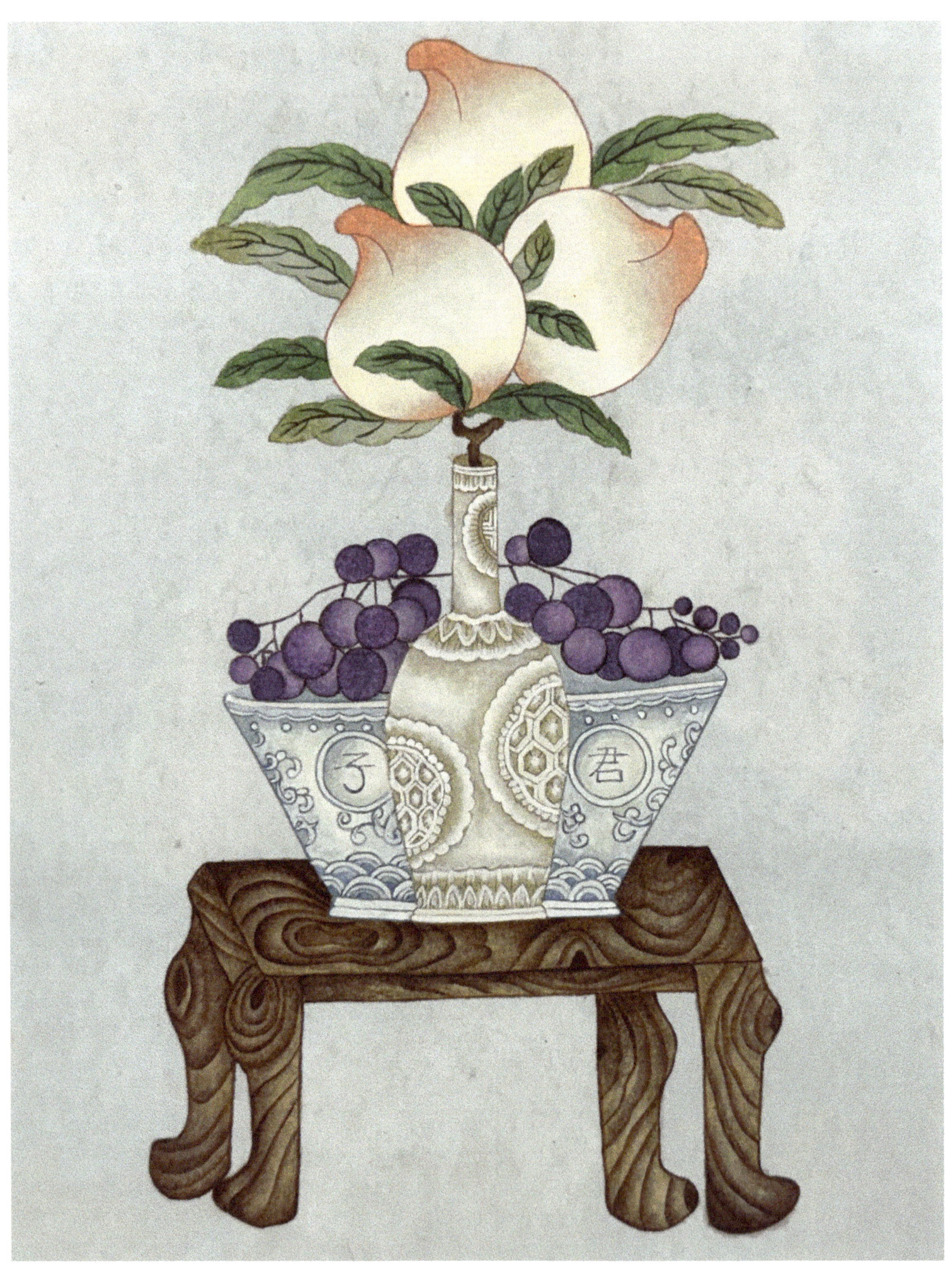

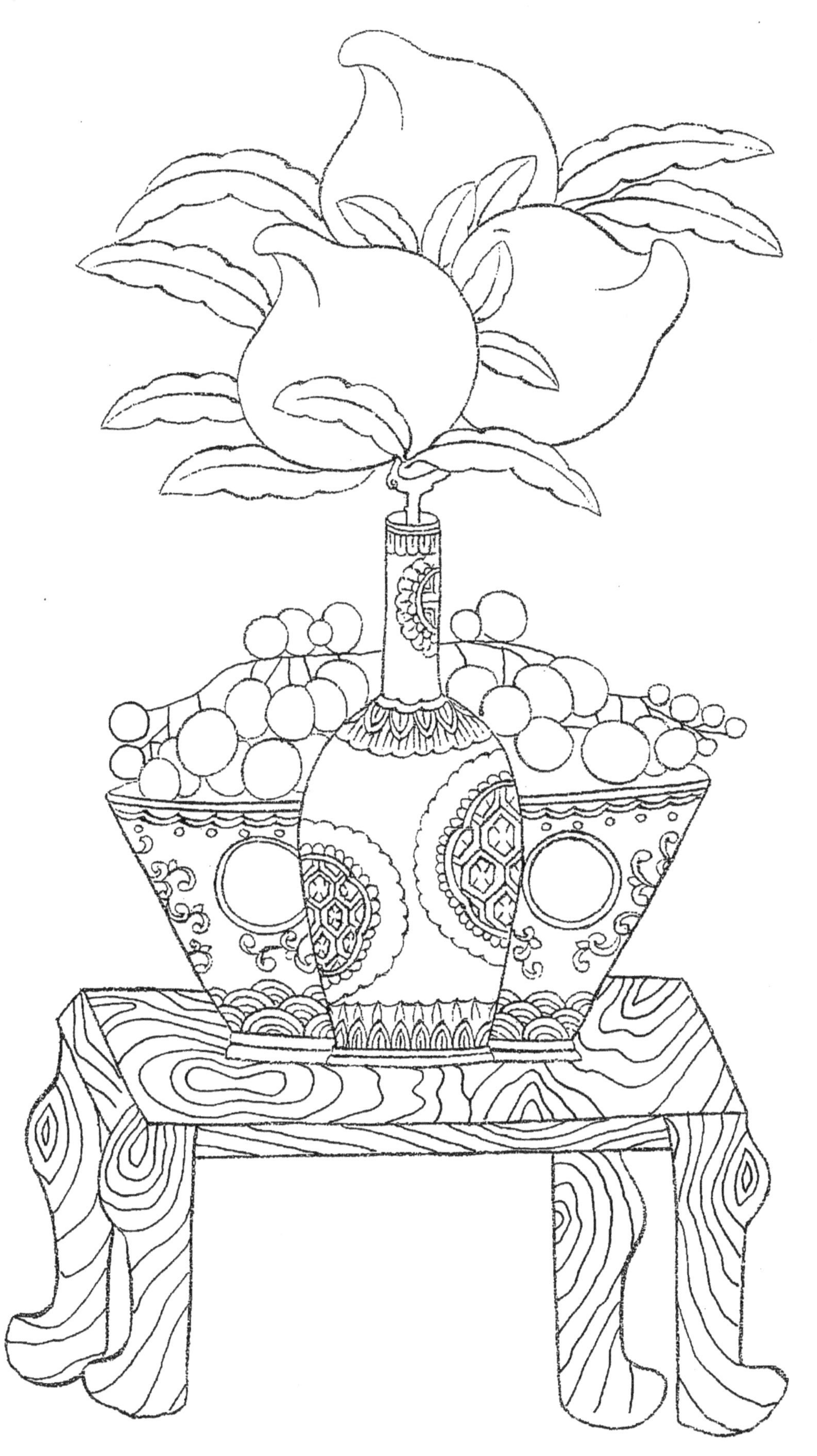

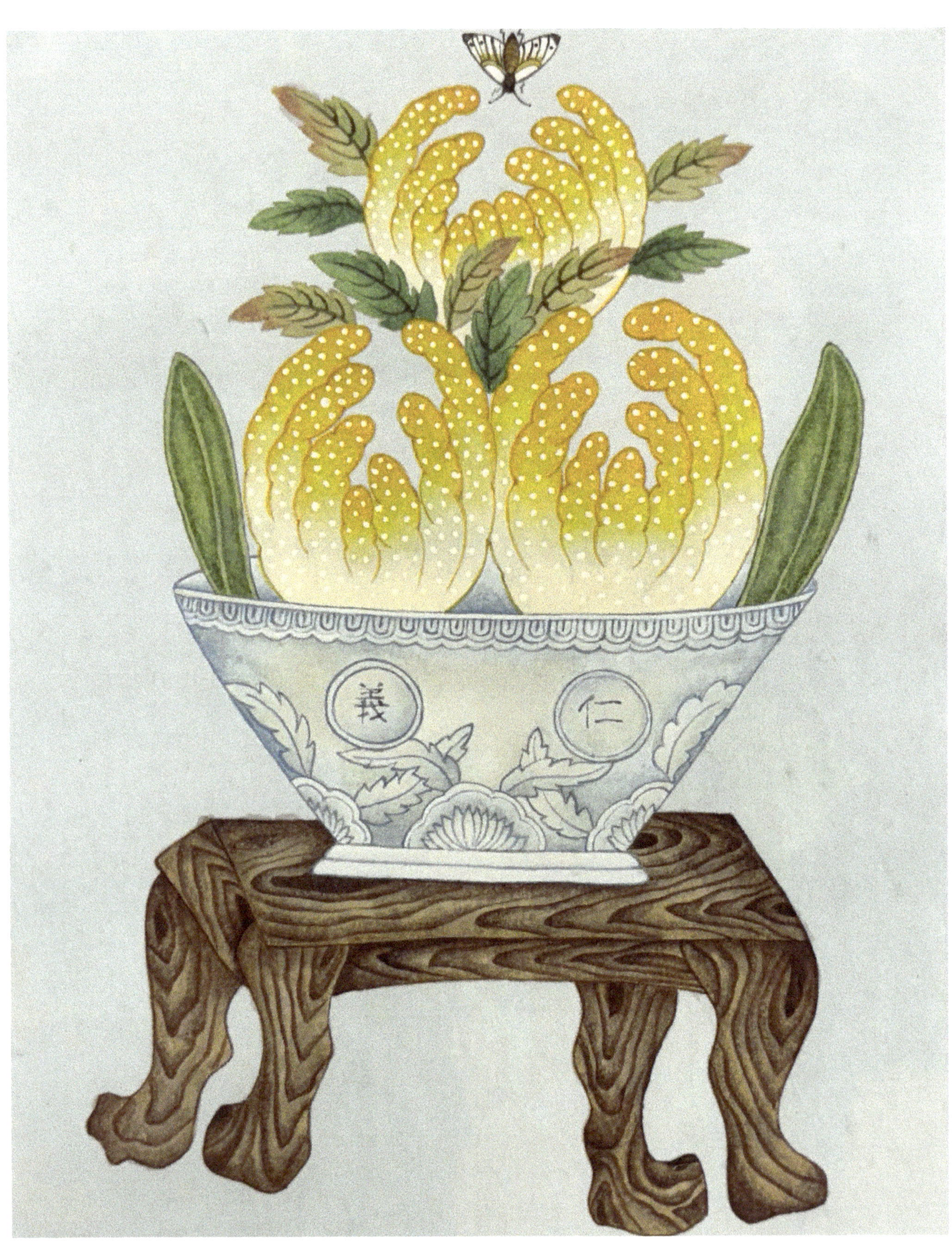

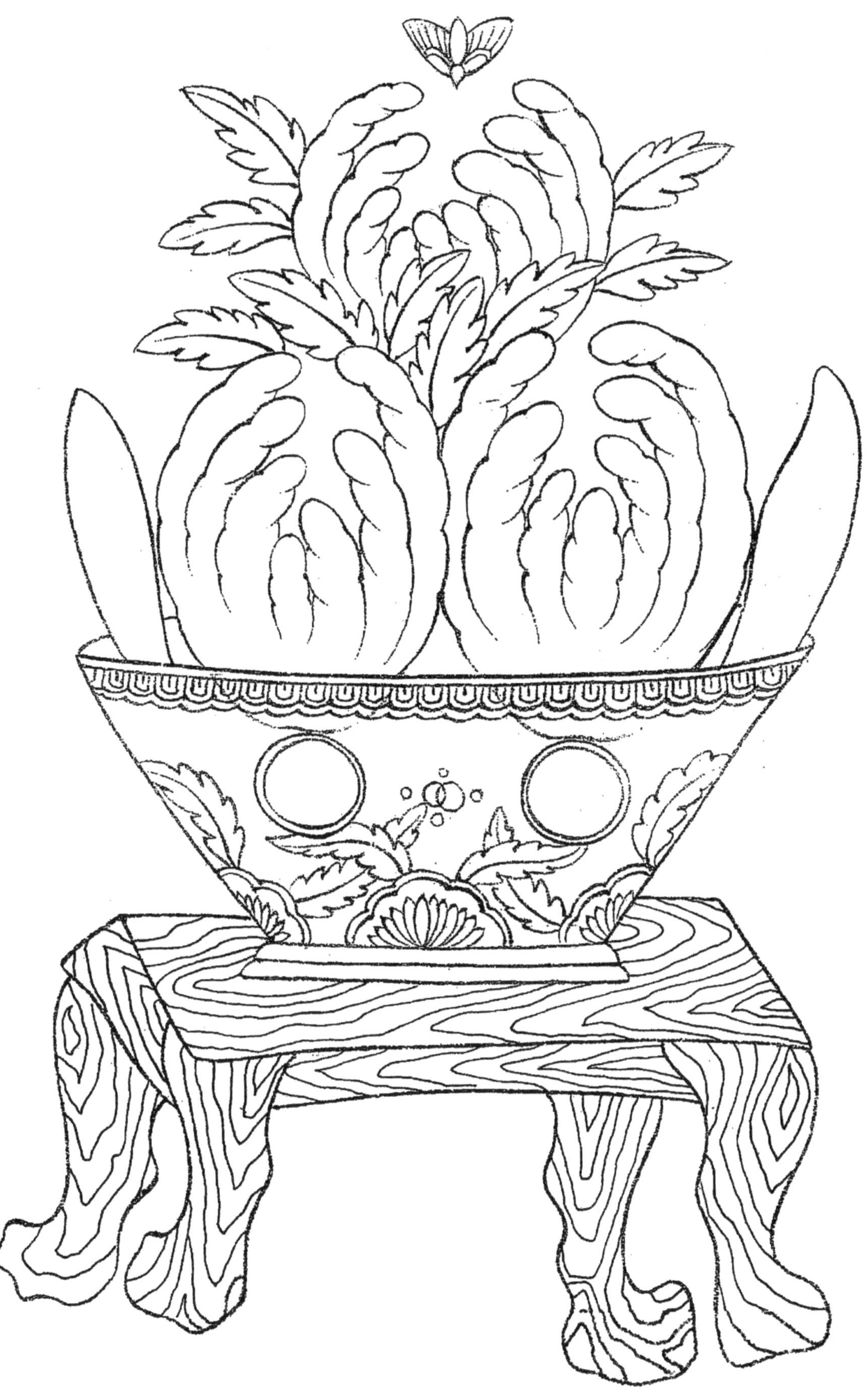

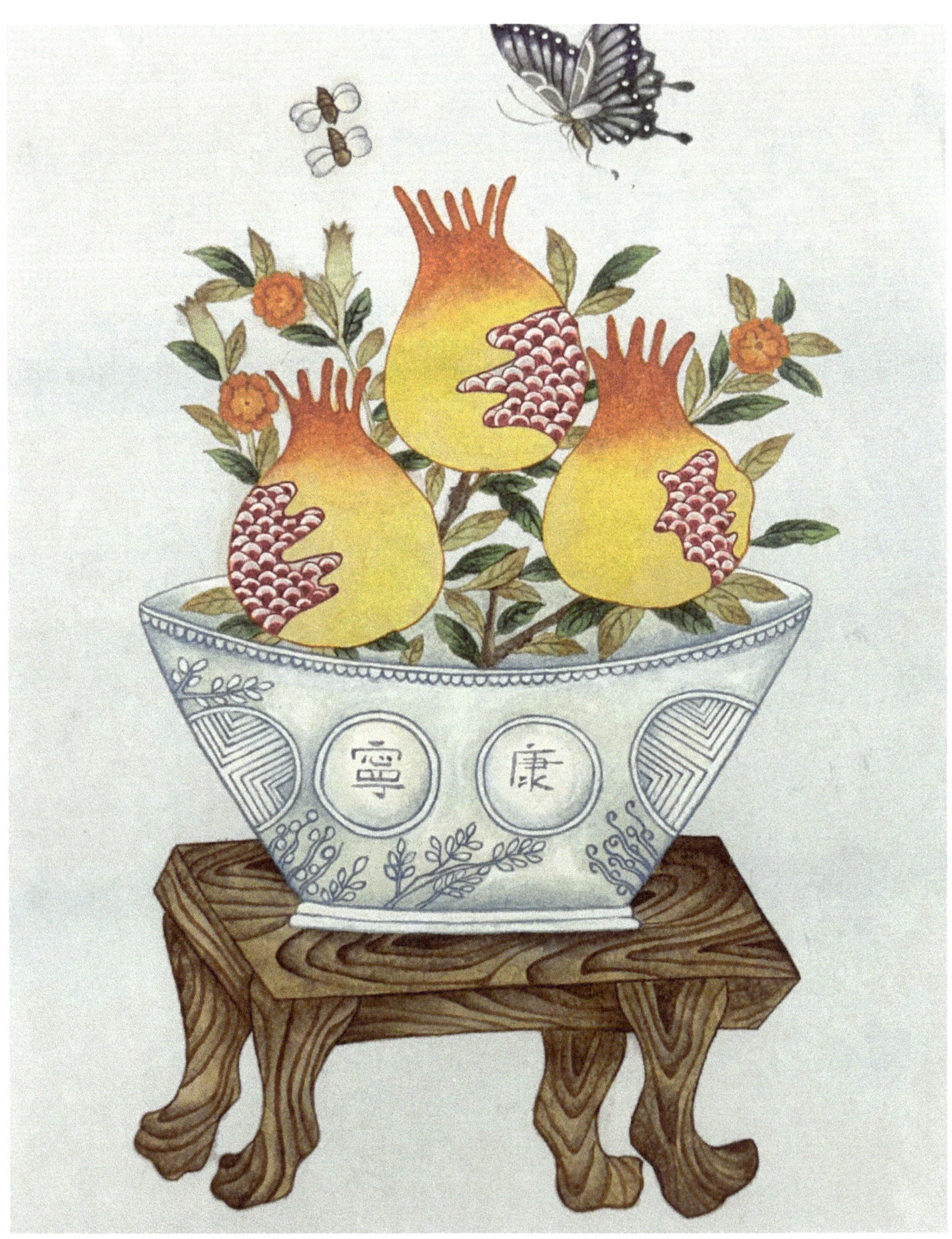寧 康

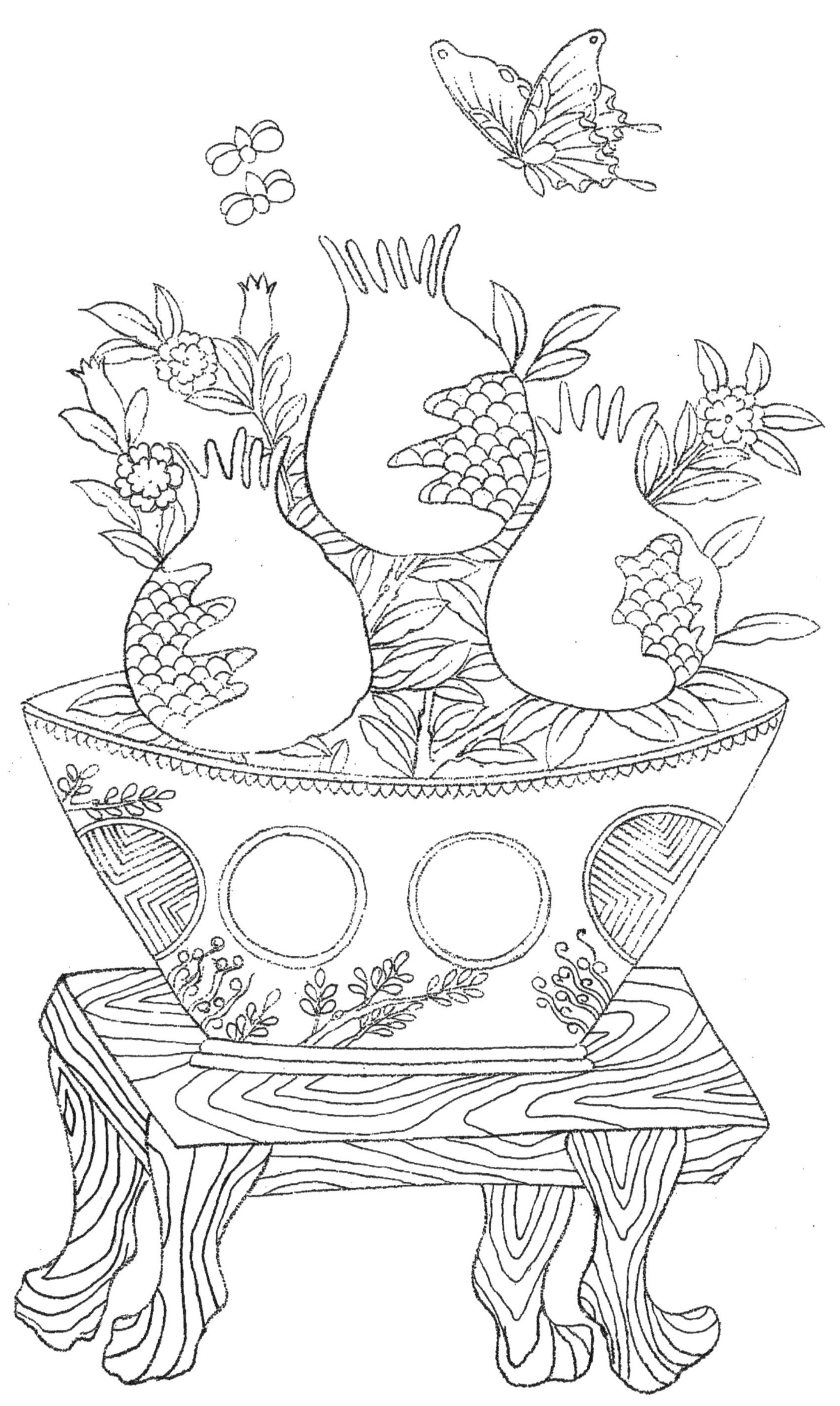

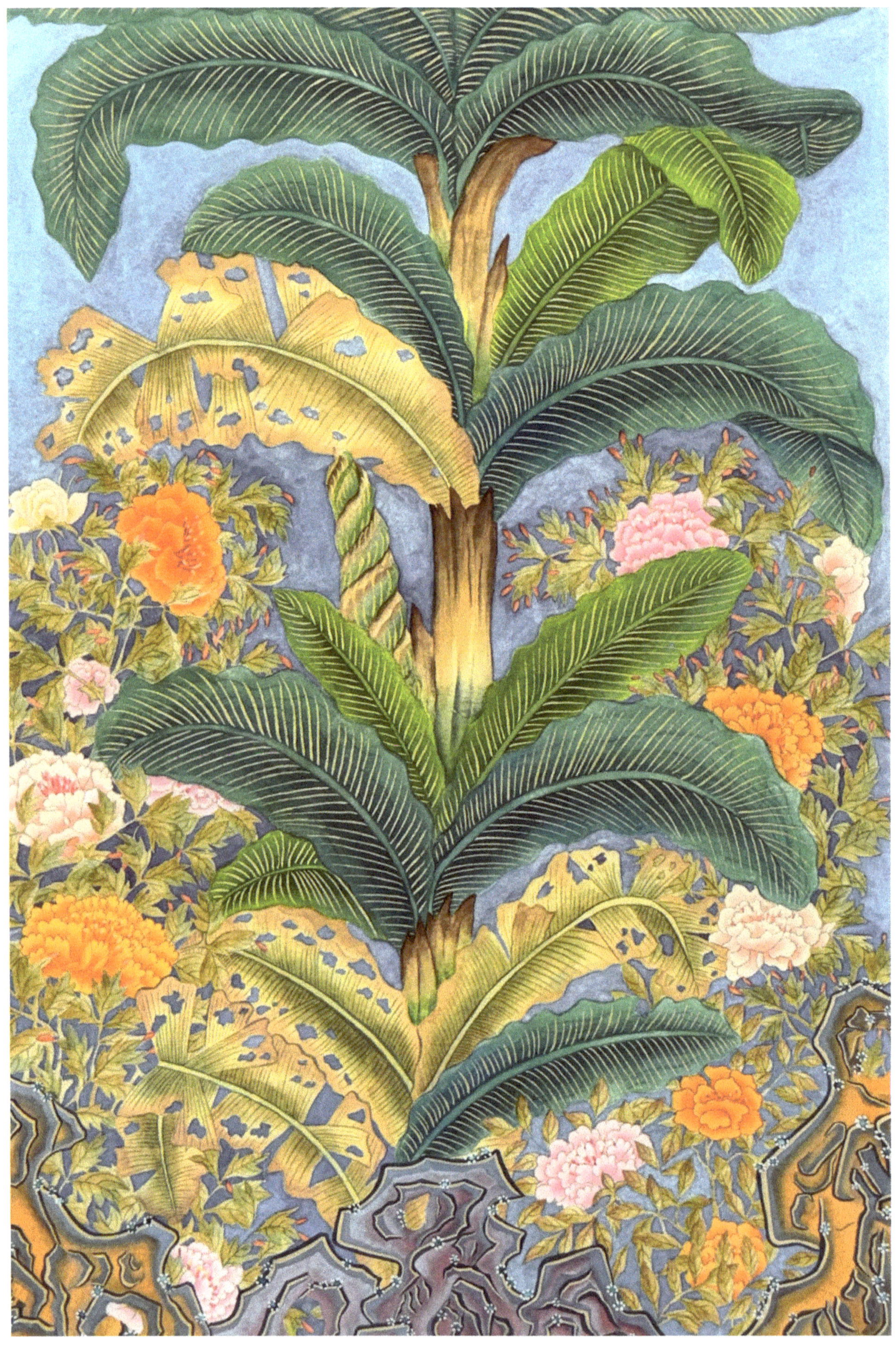

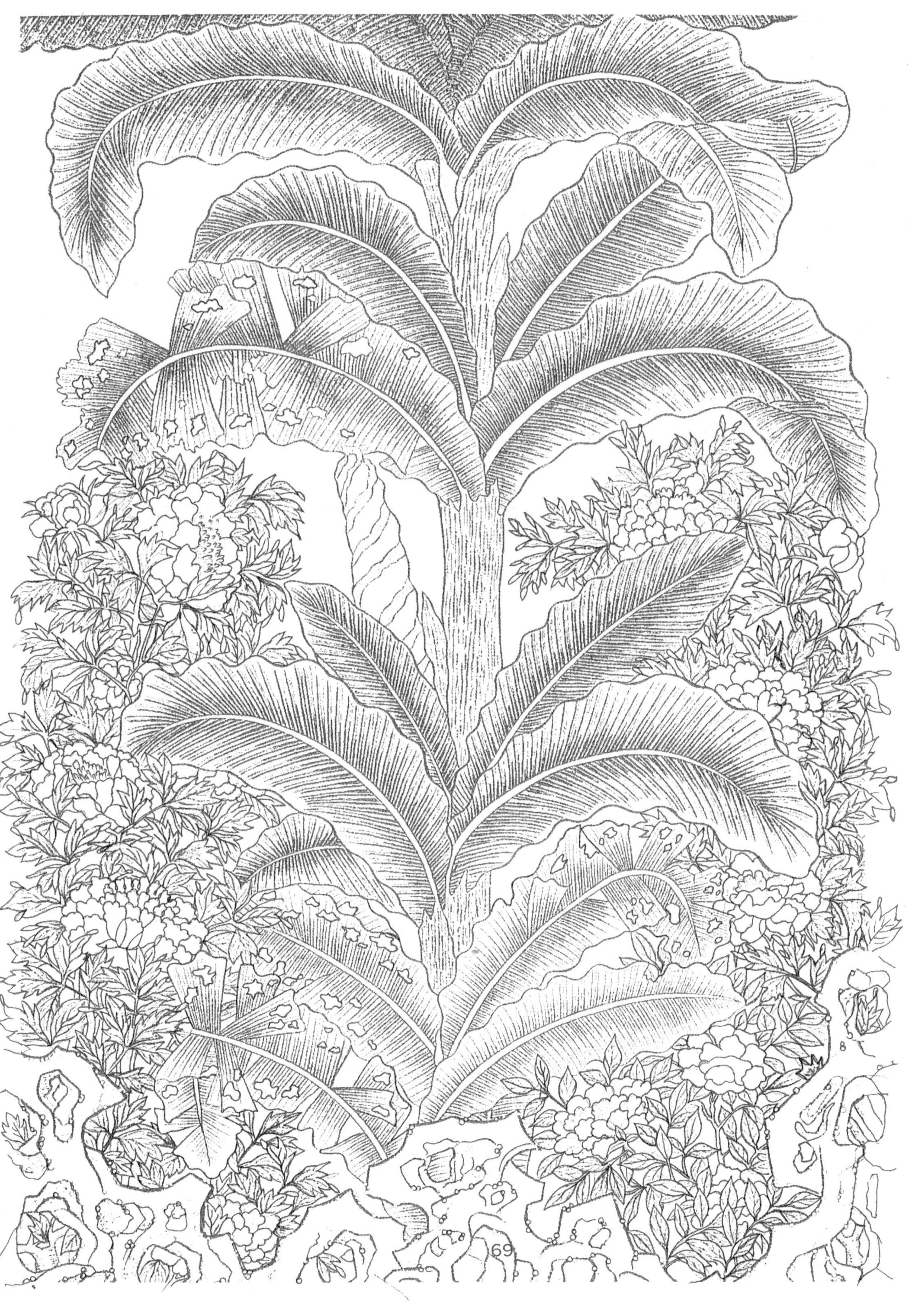

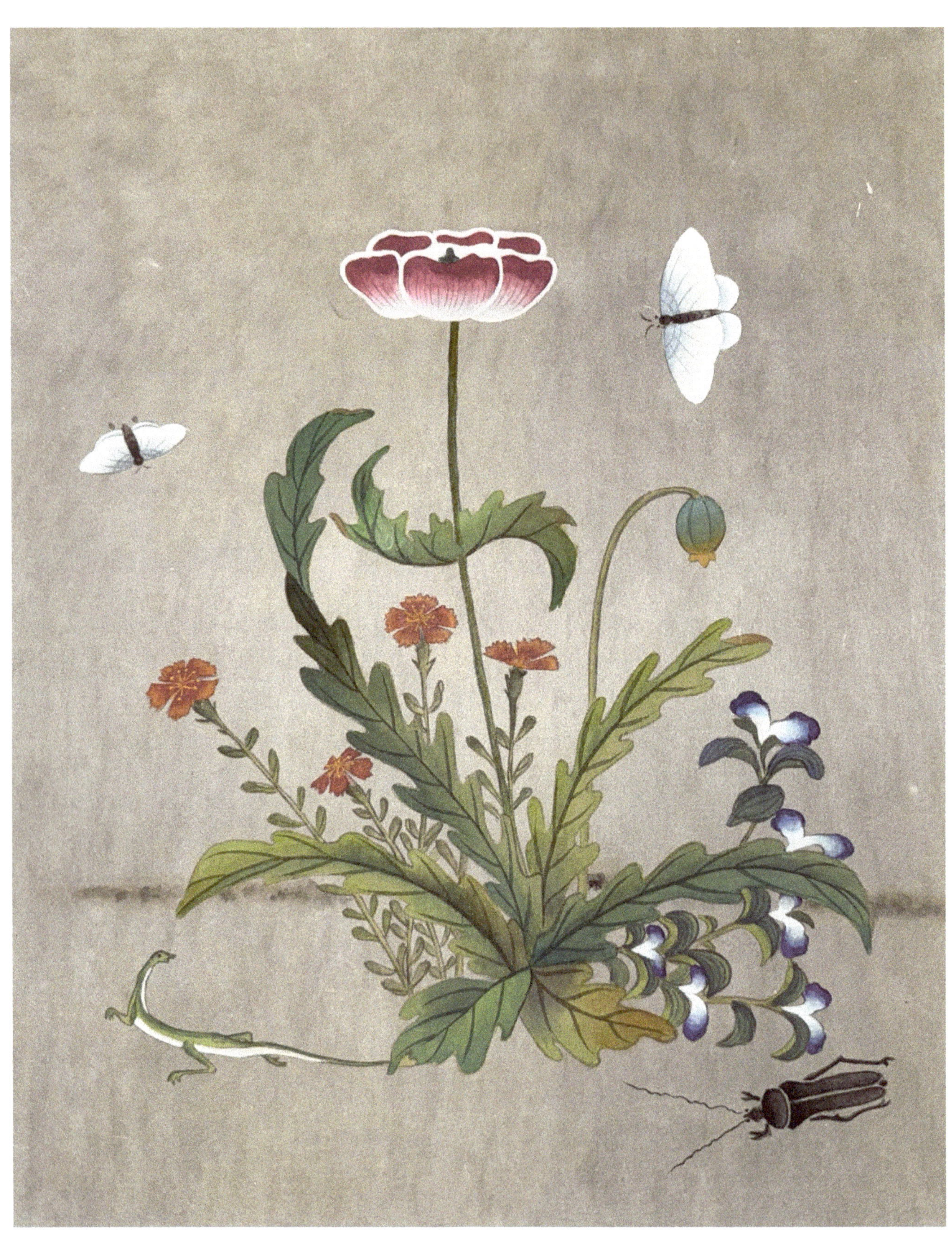

Original Artist: Shin Saim-Dang
Recoloration: Author

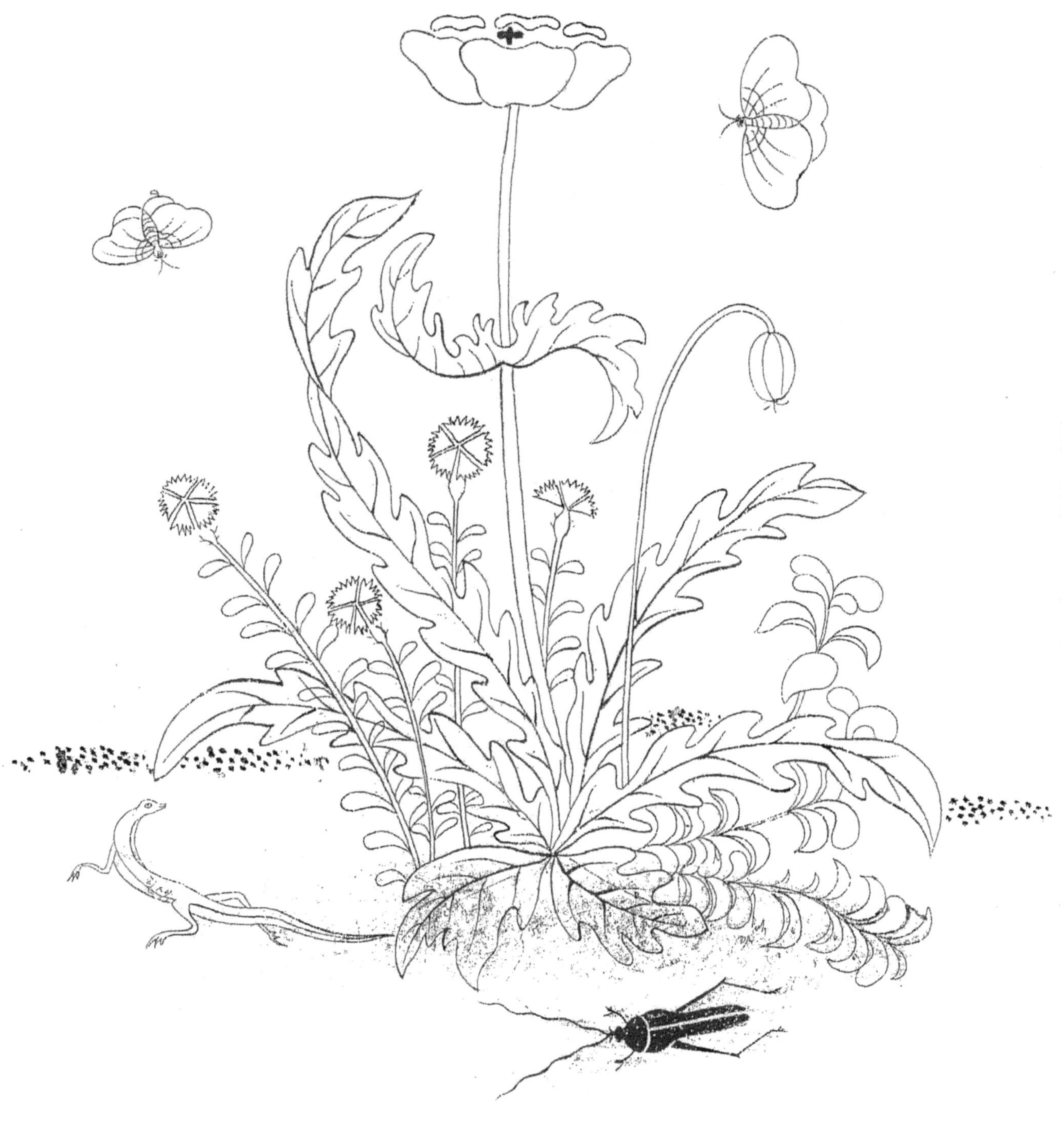

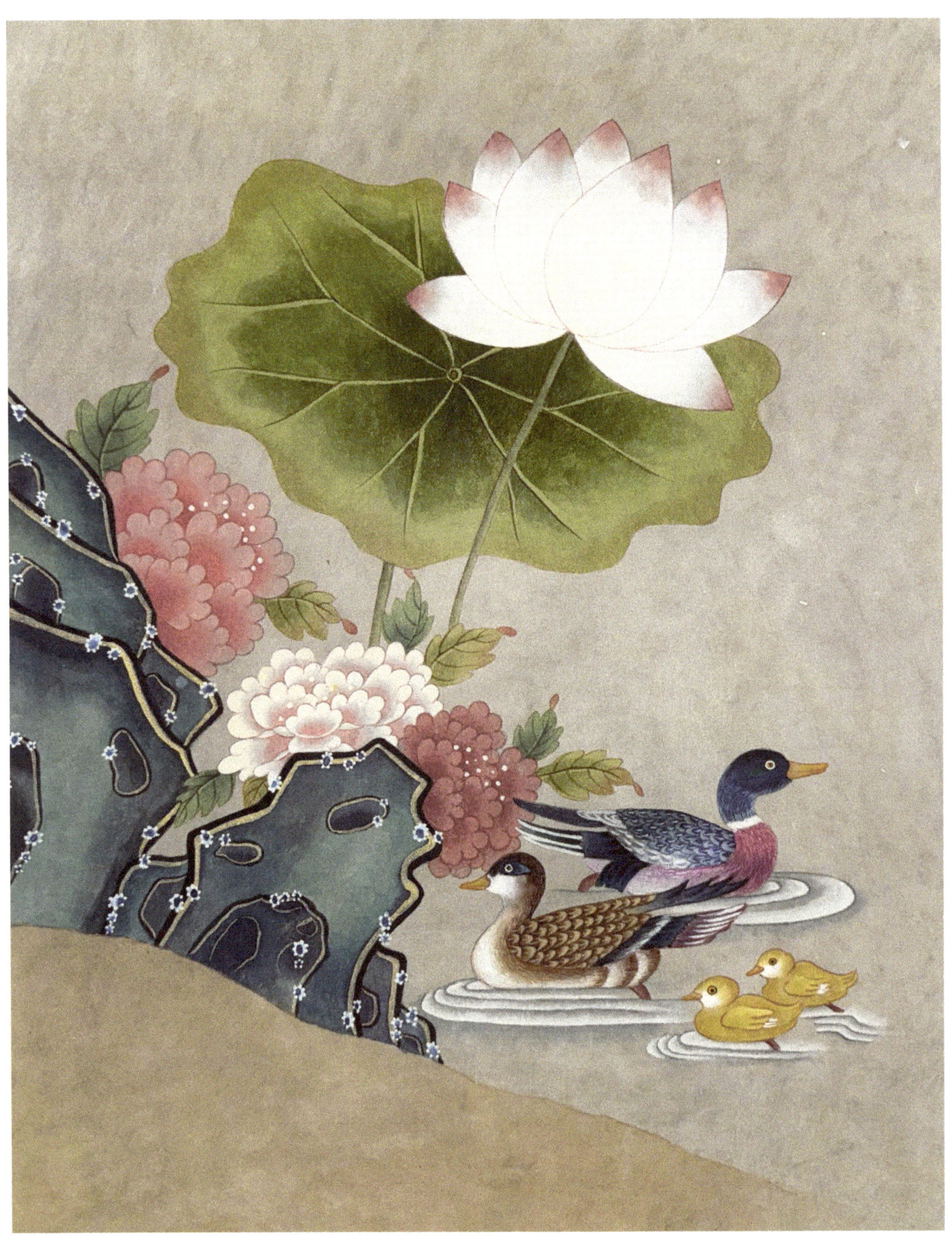

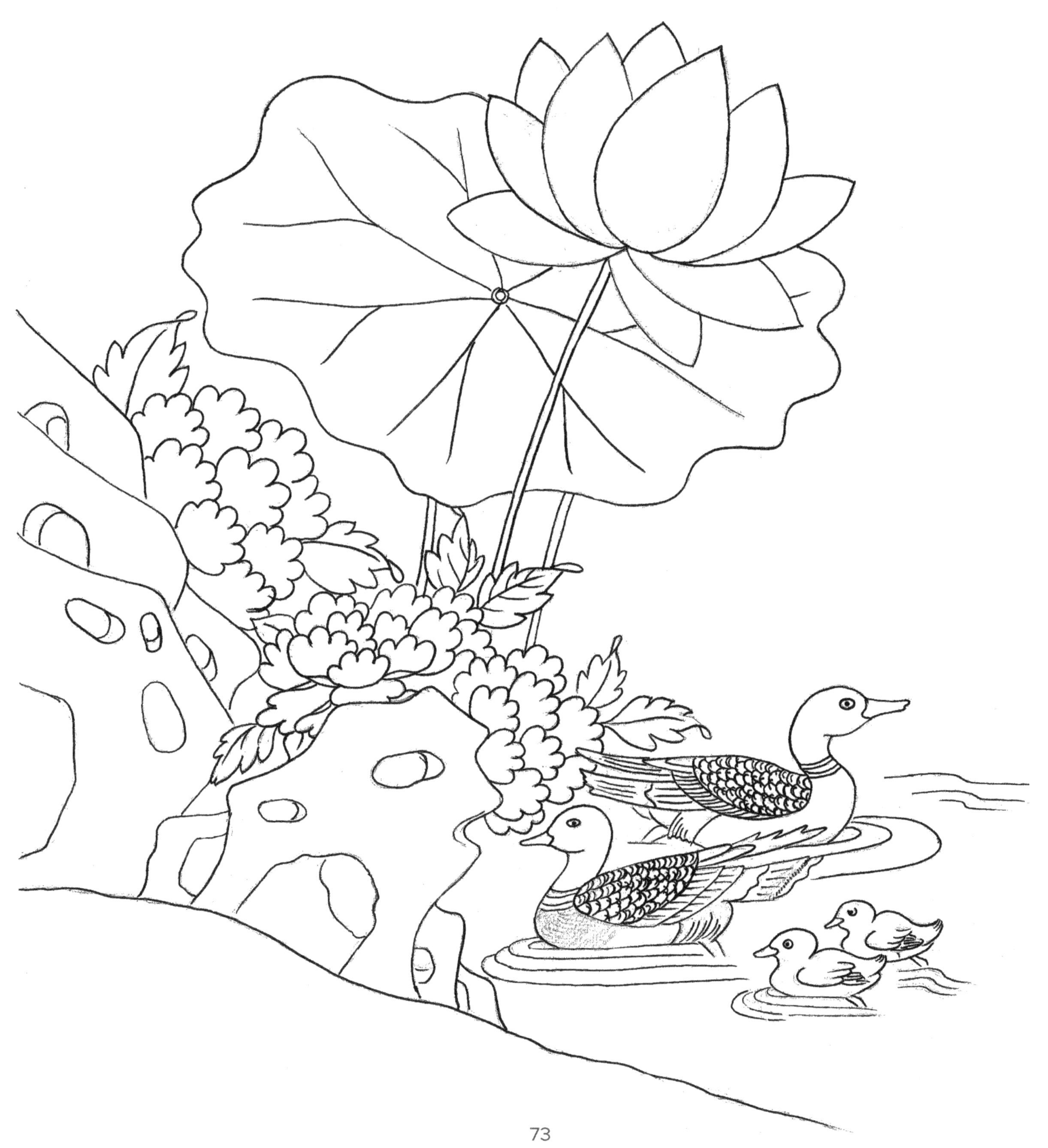

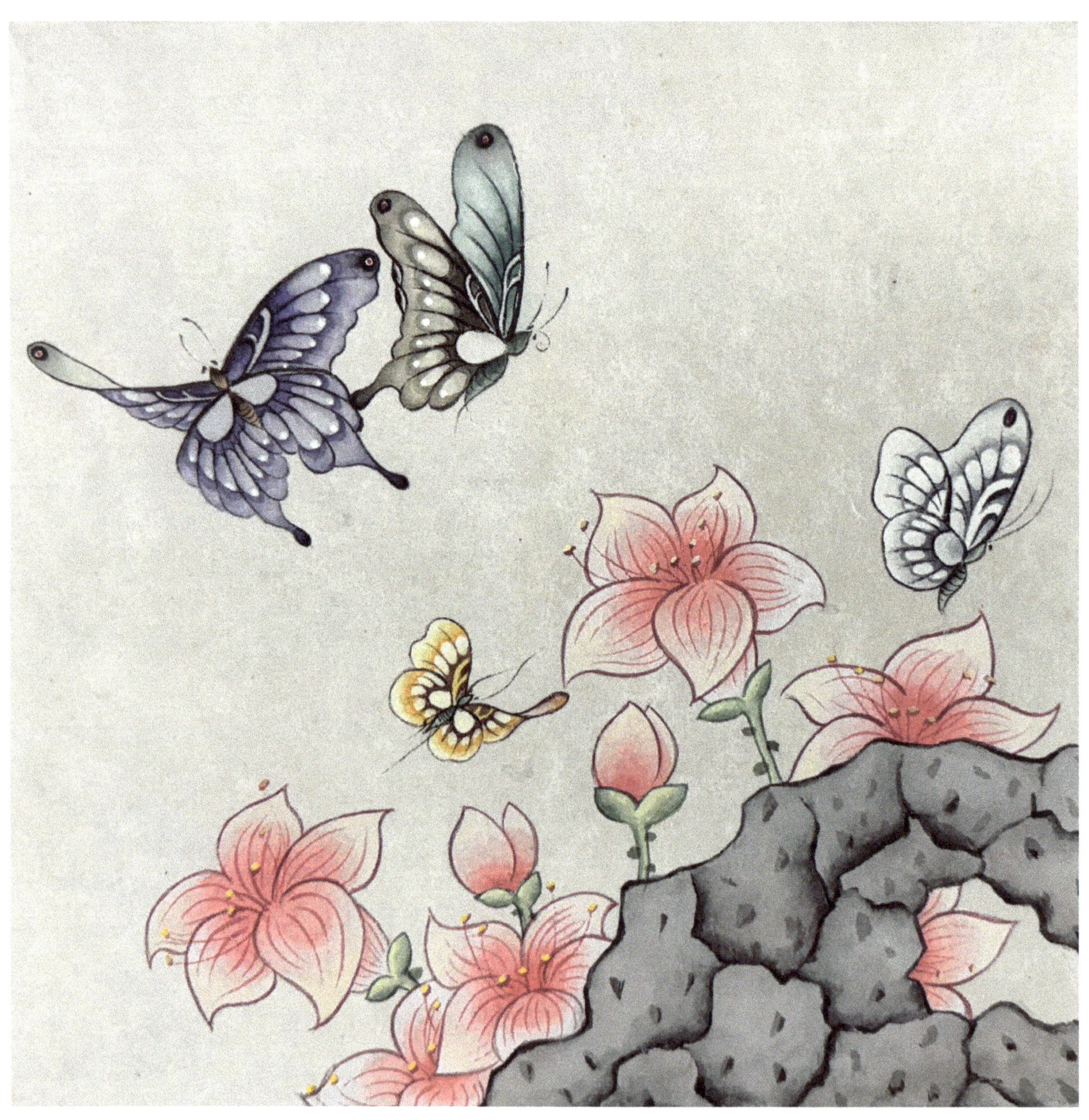

Original Artist: Hye-Ryung Suk

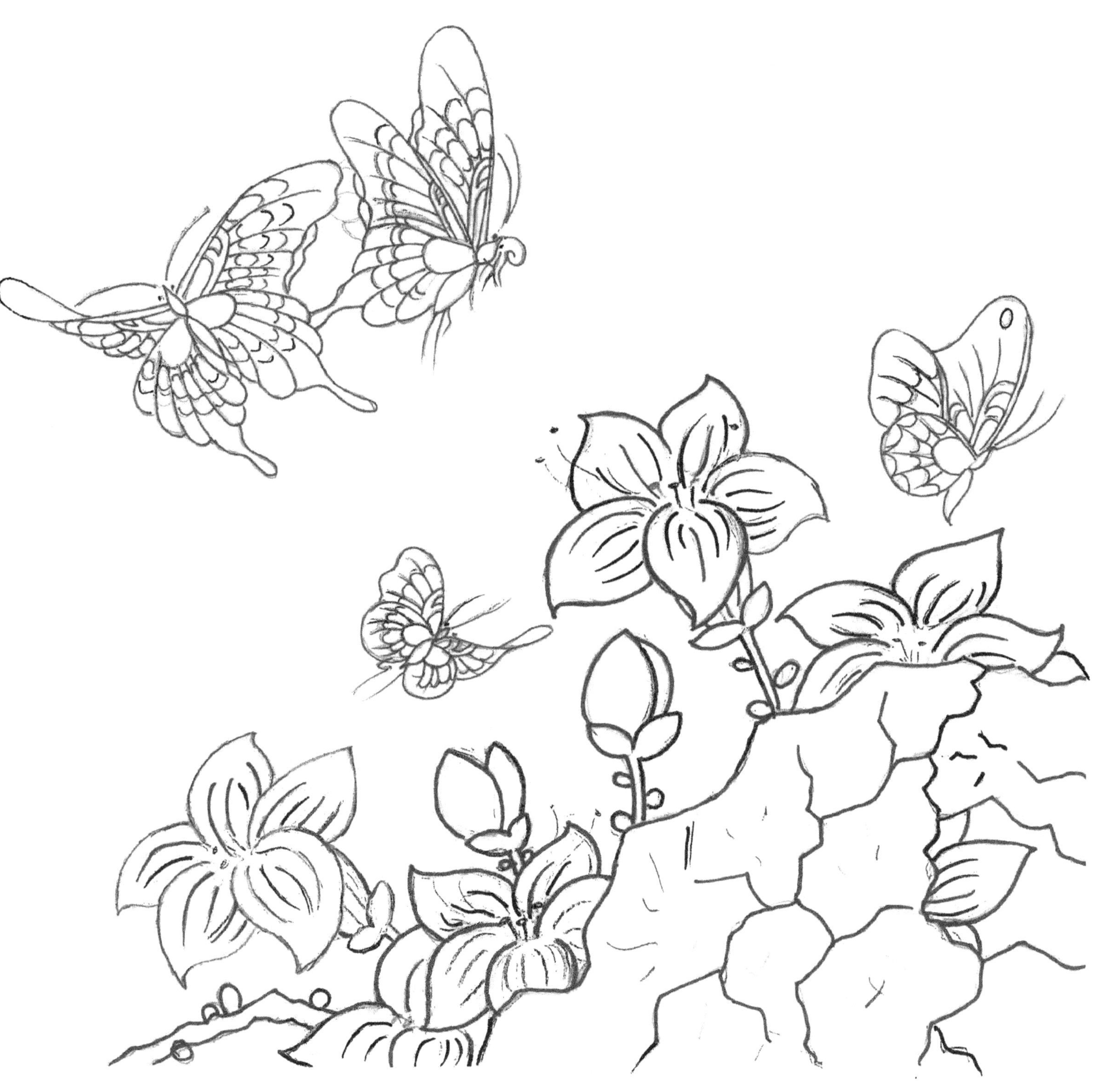

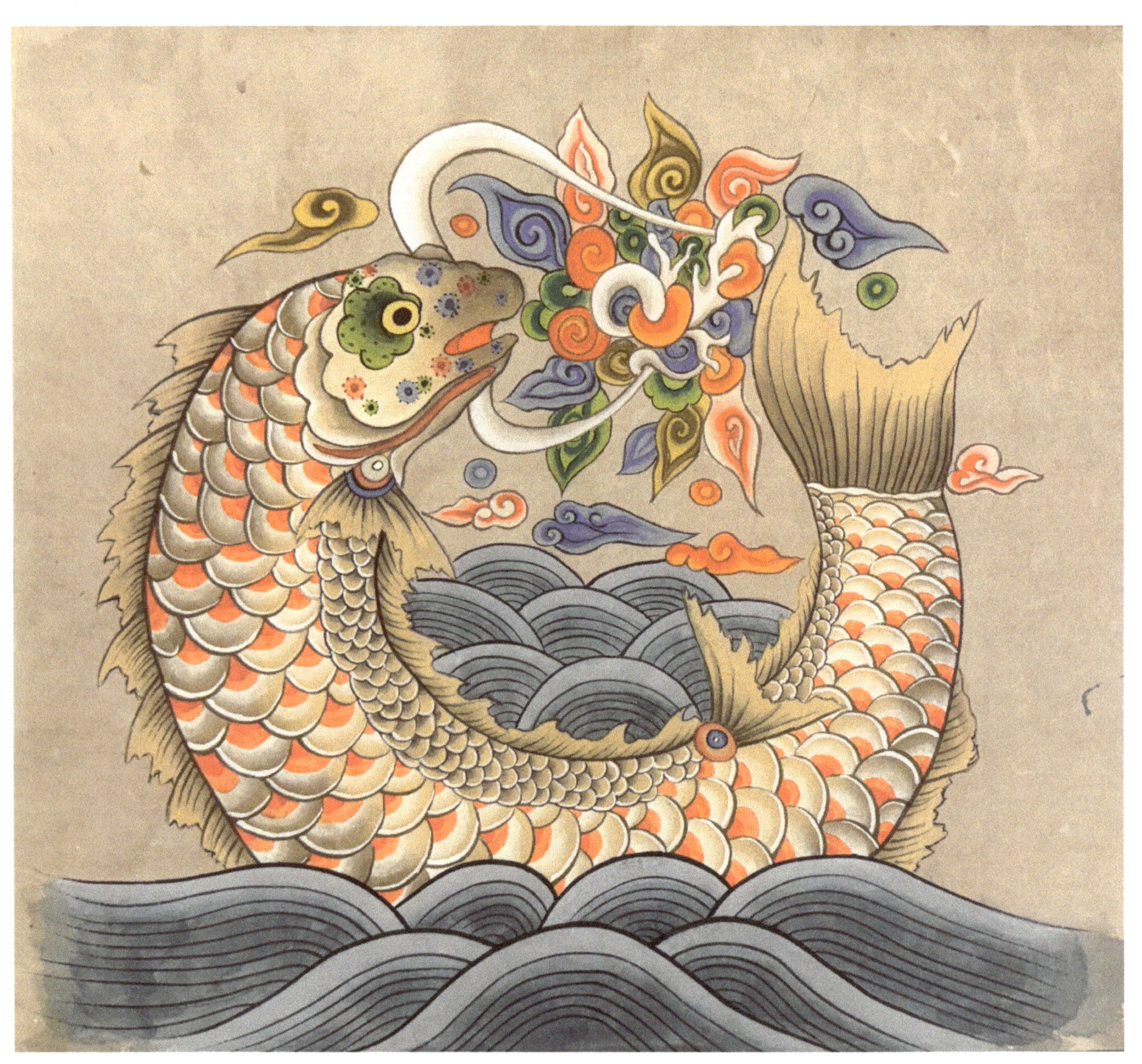

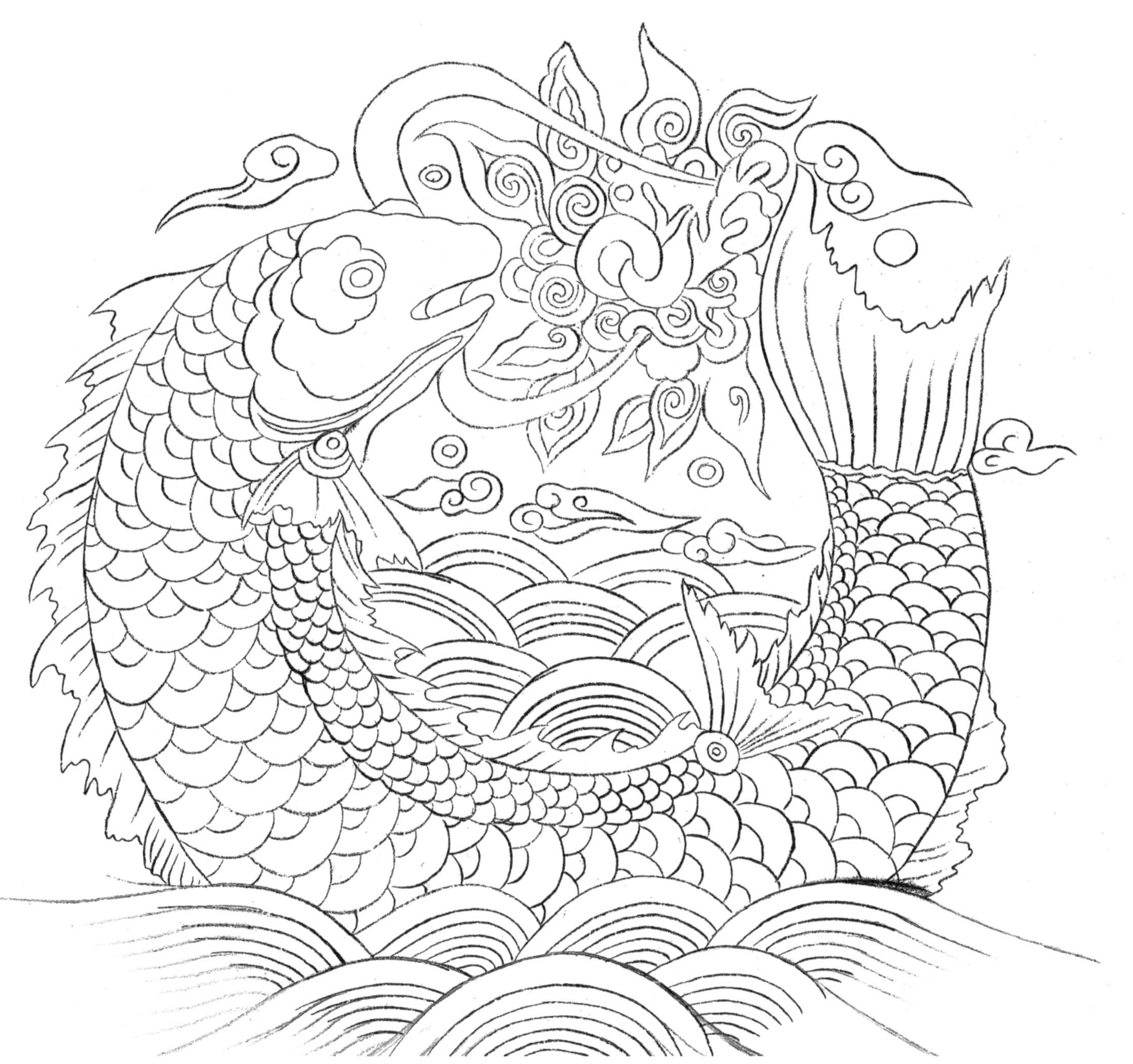

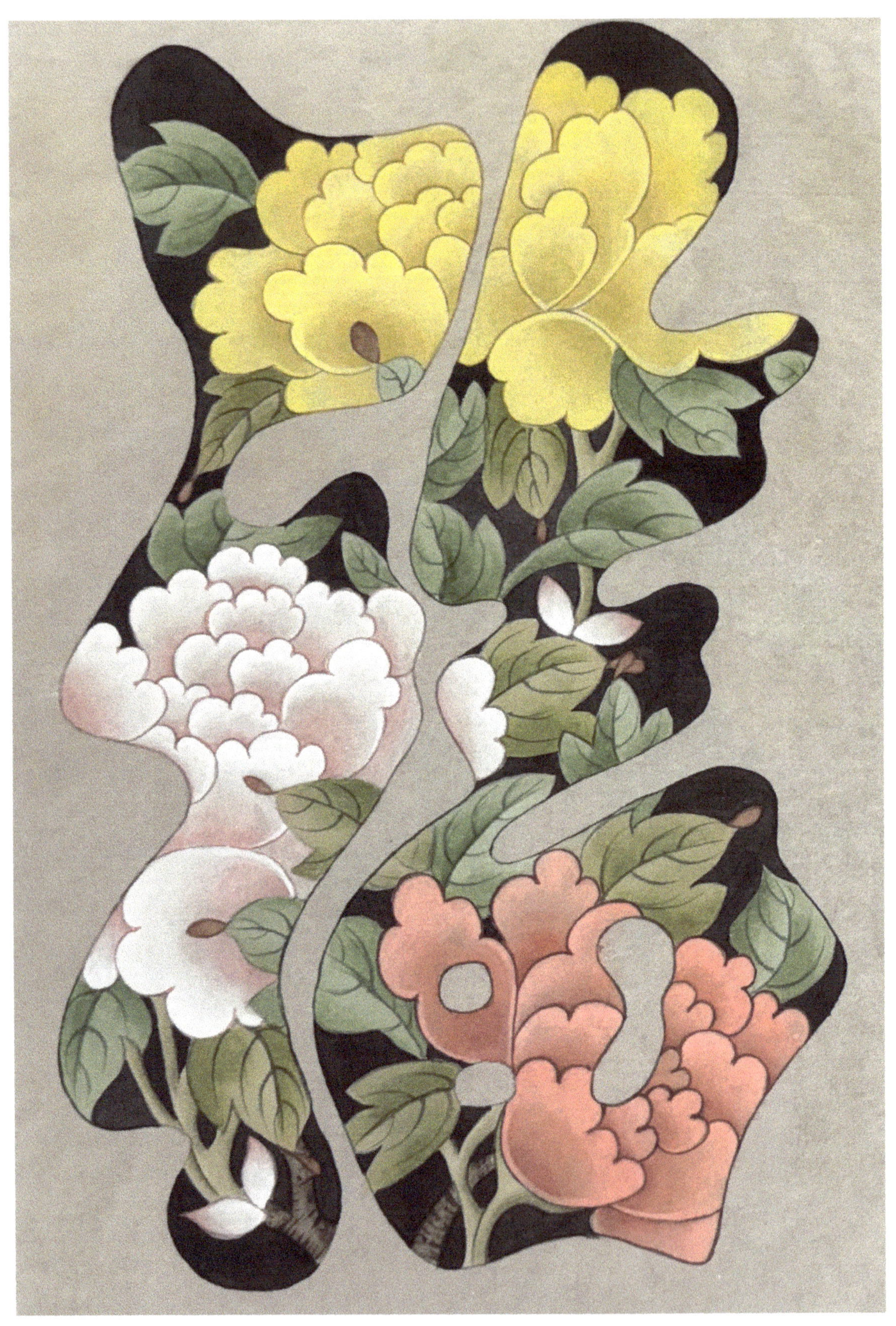

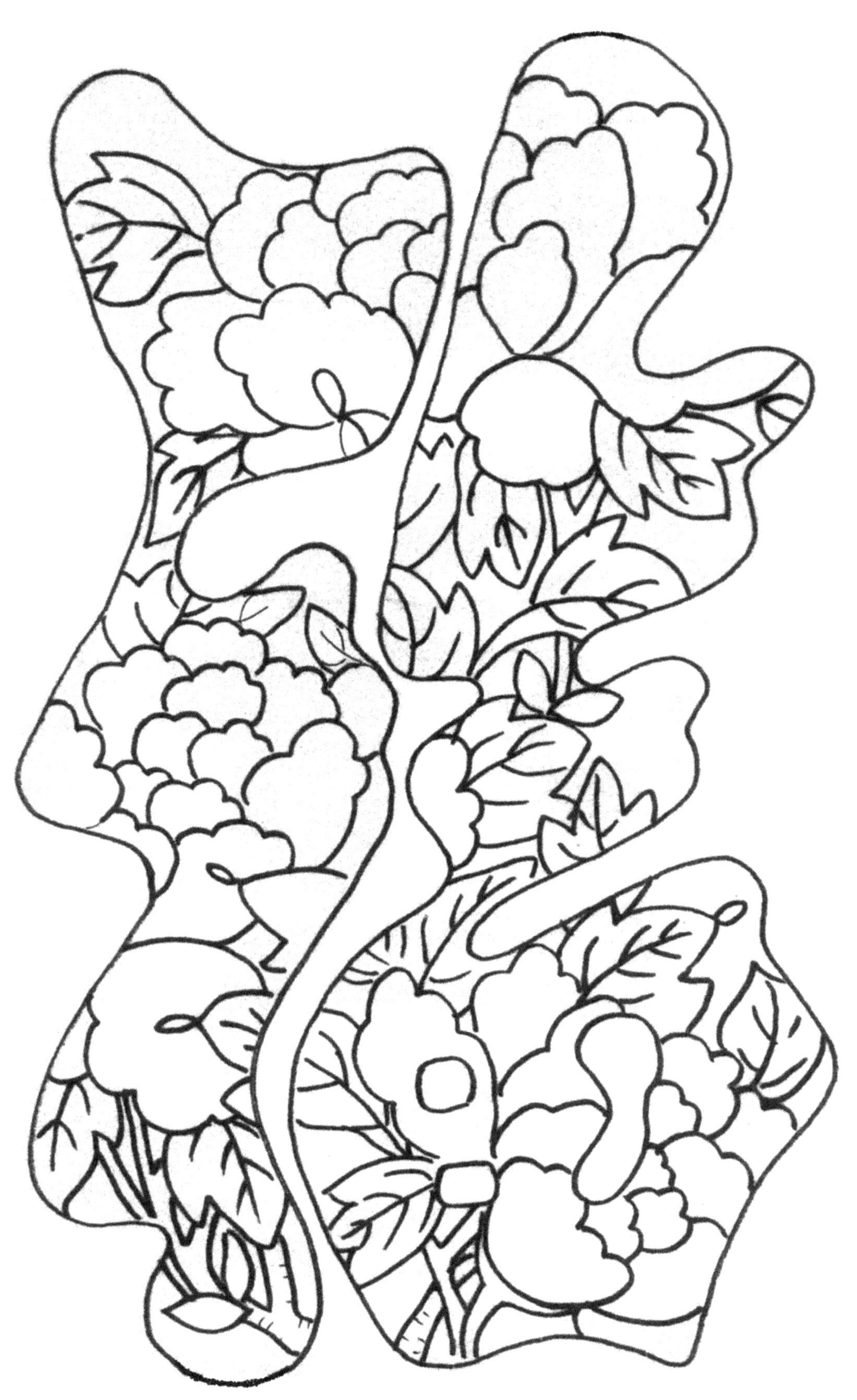

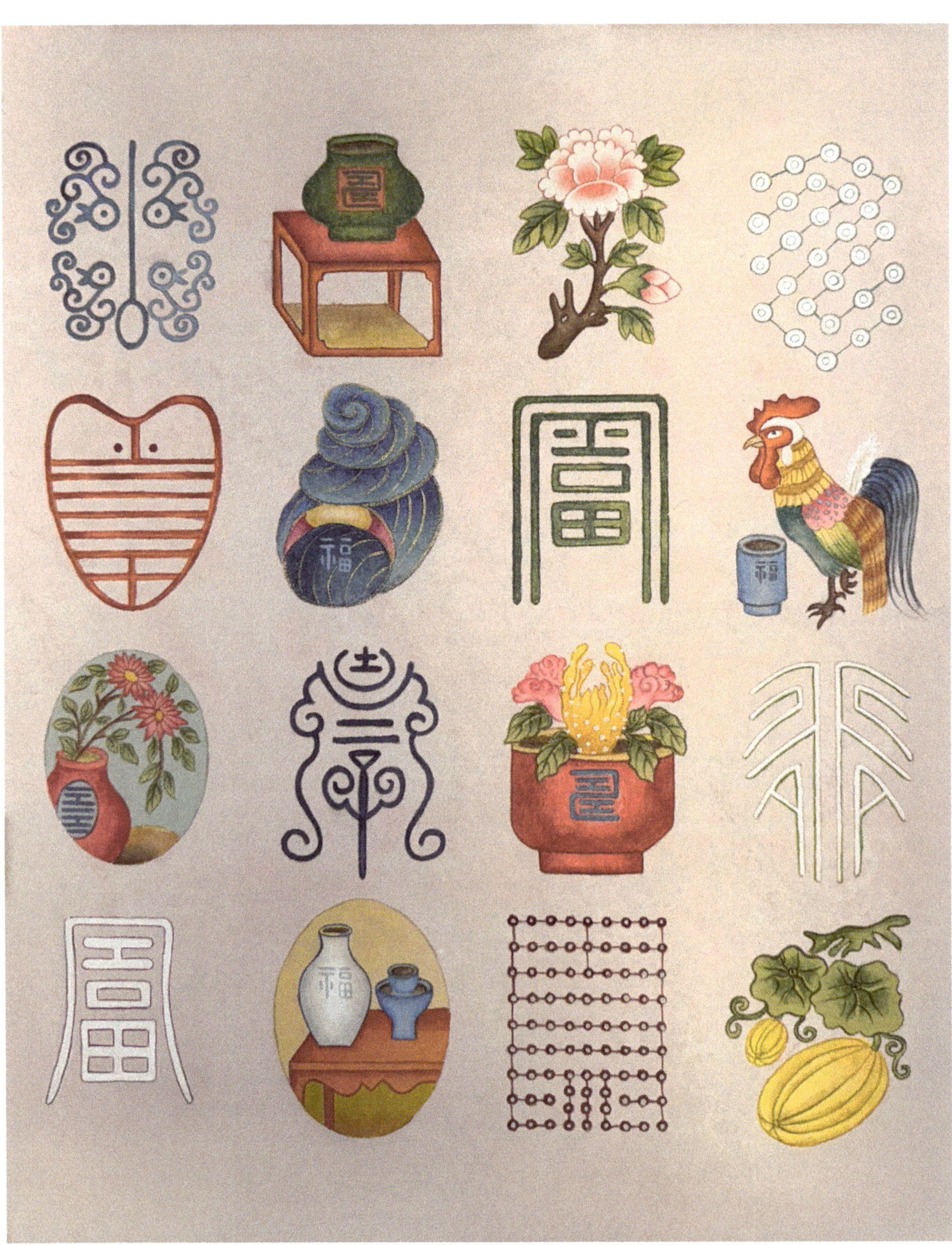

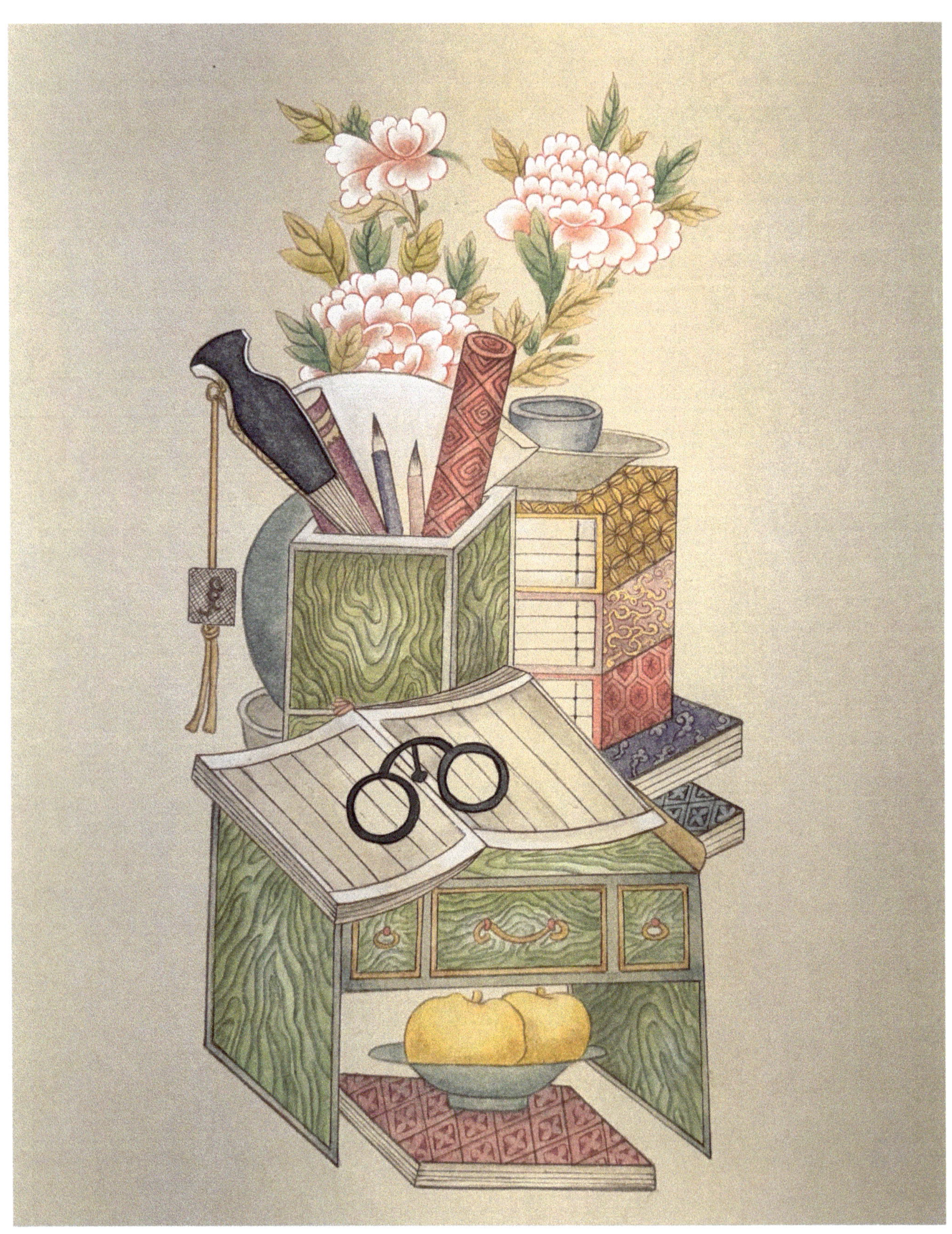

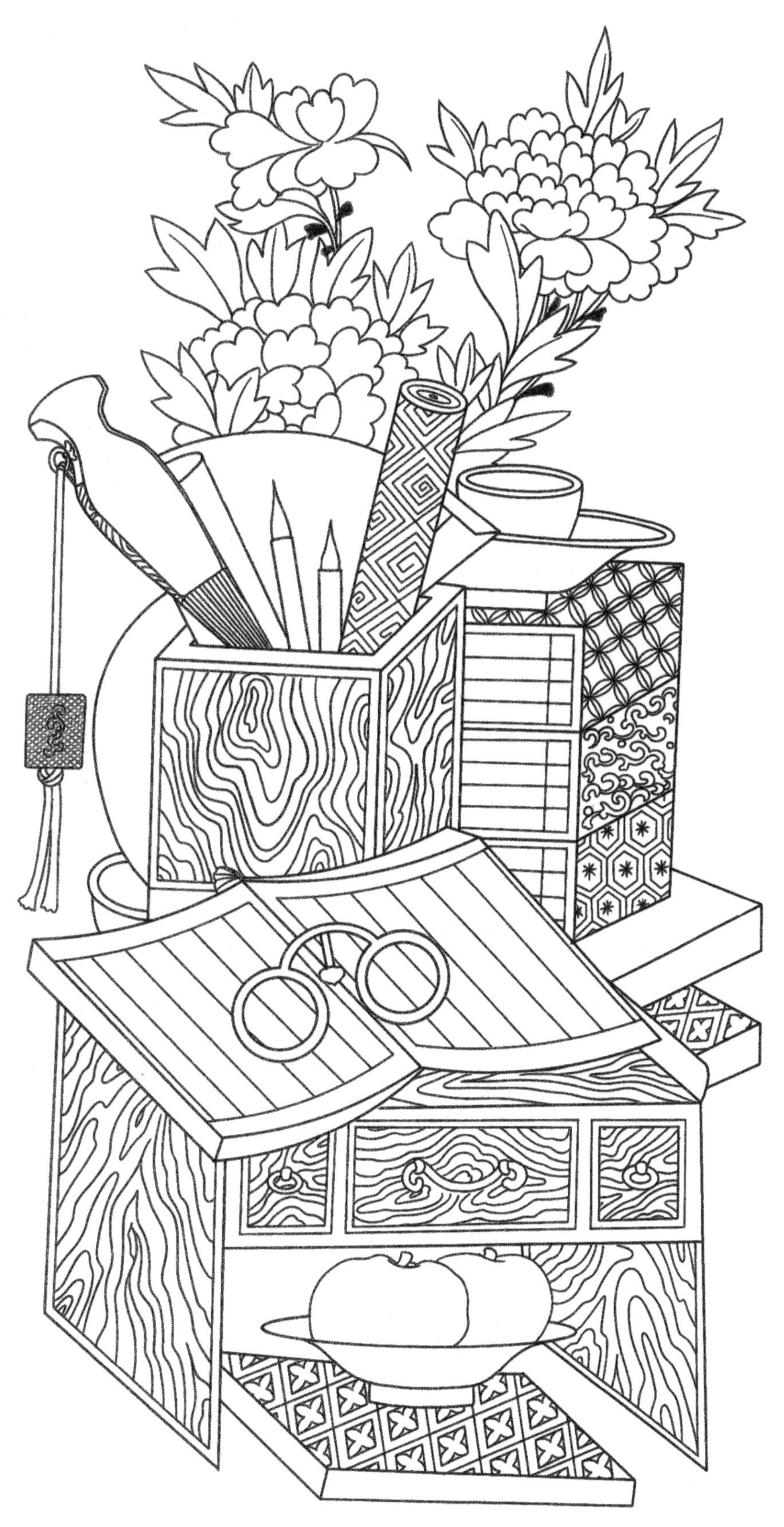

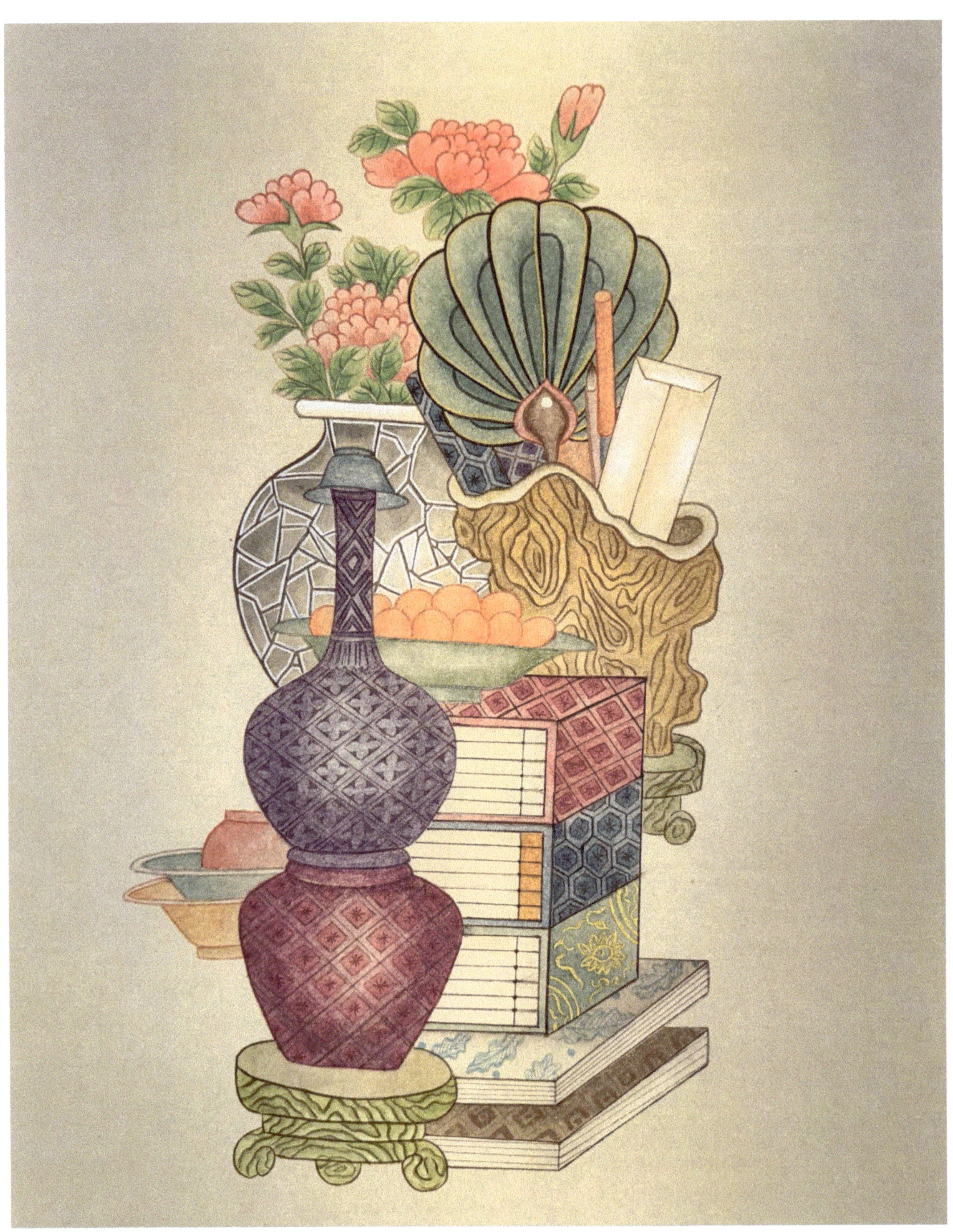

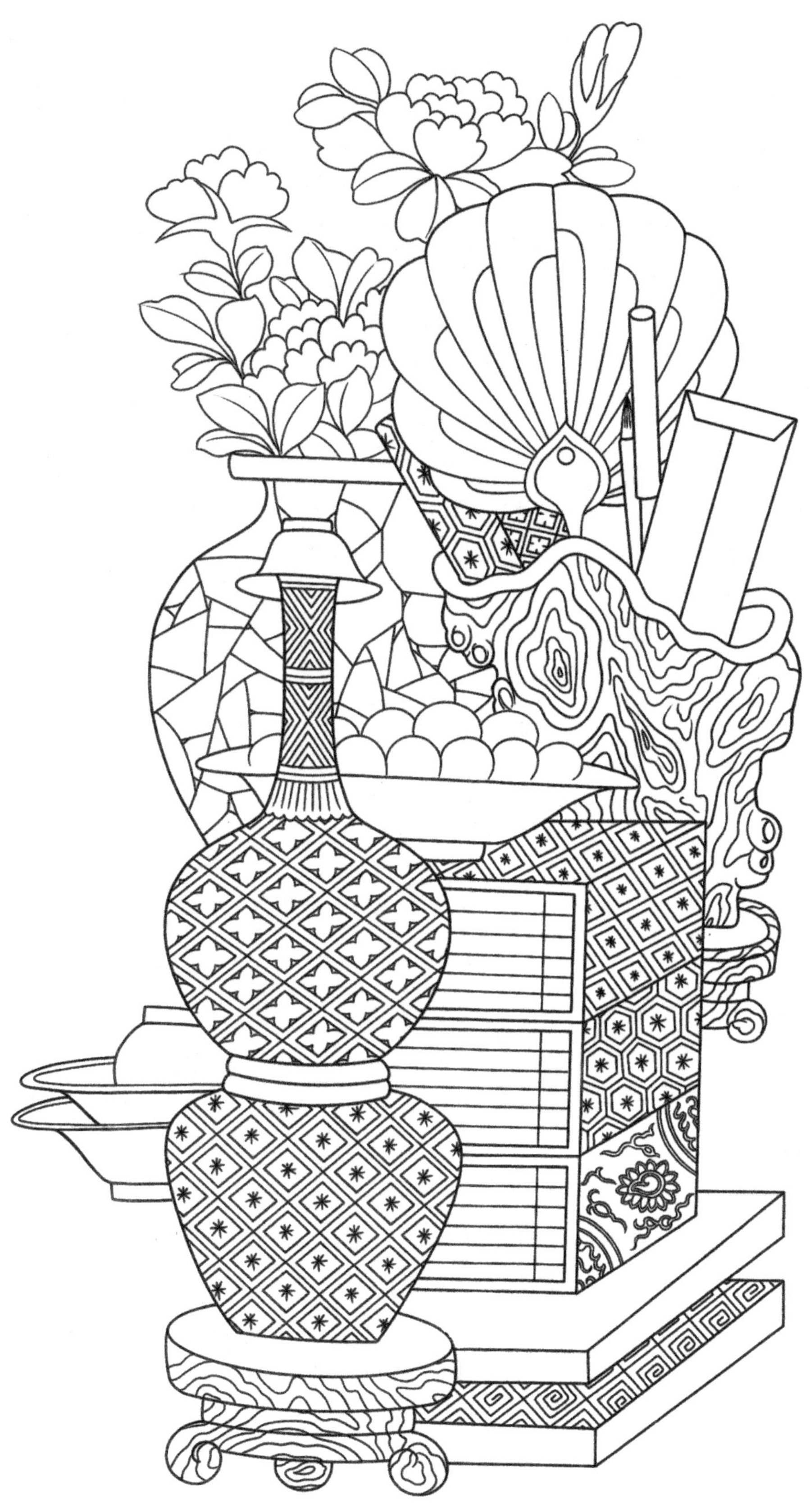

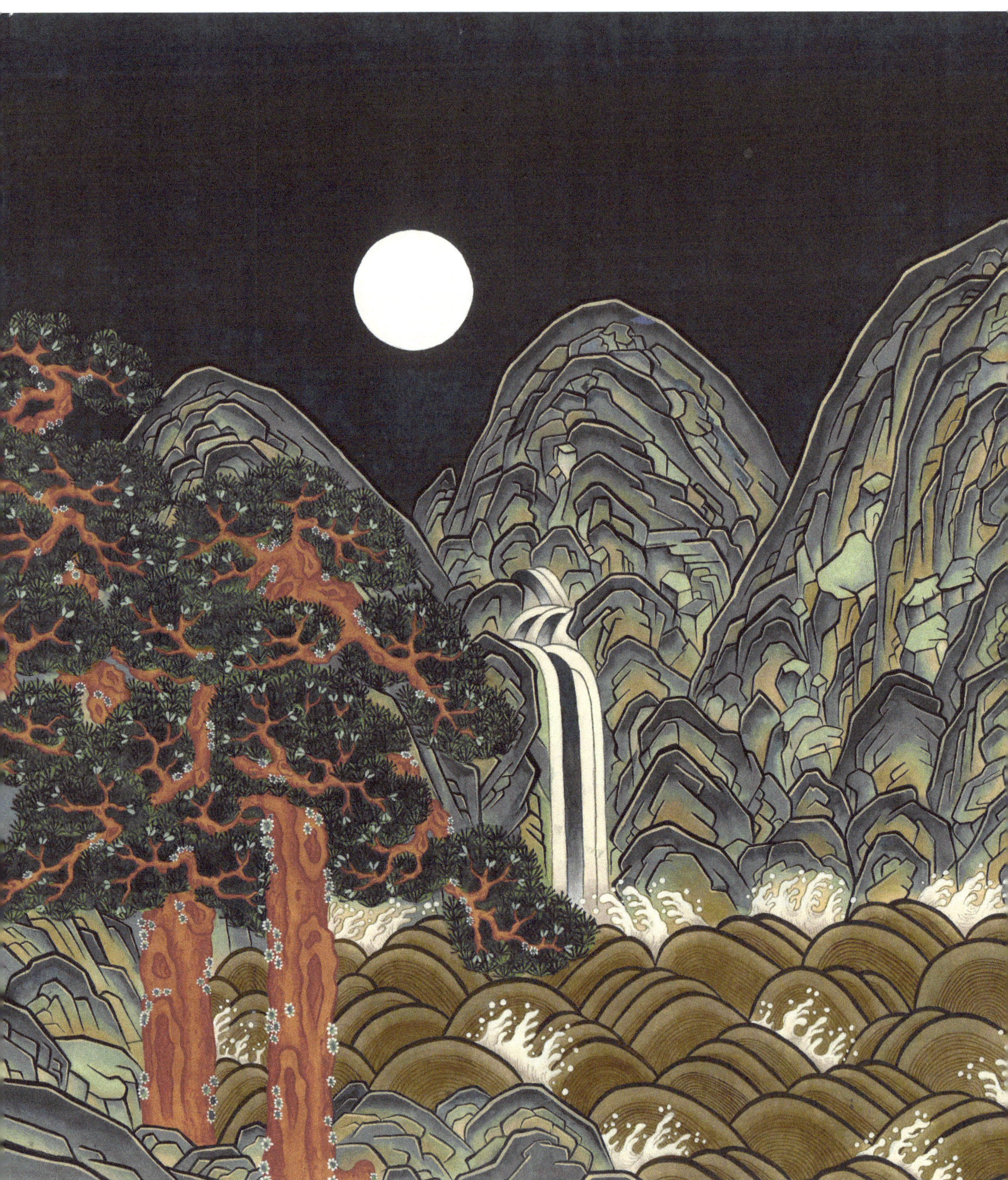

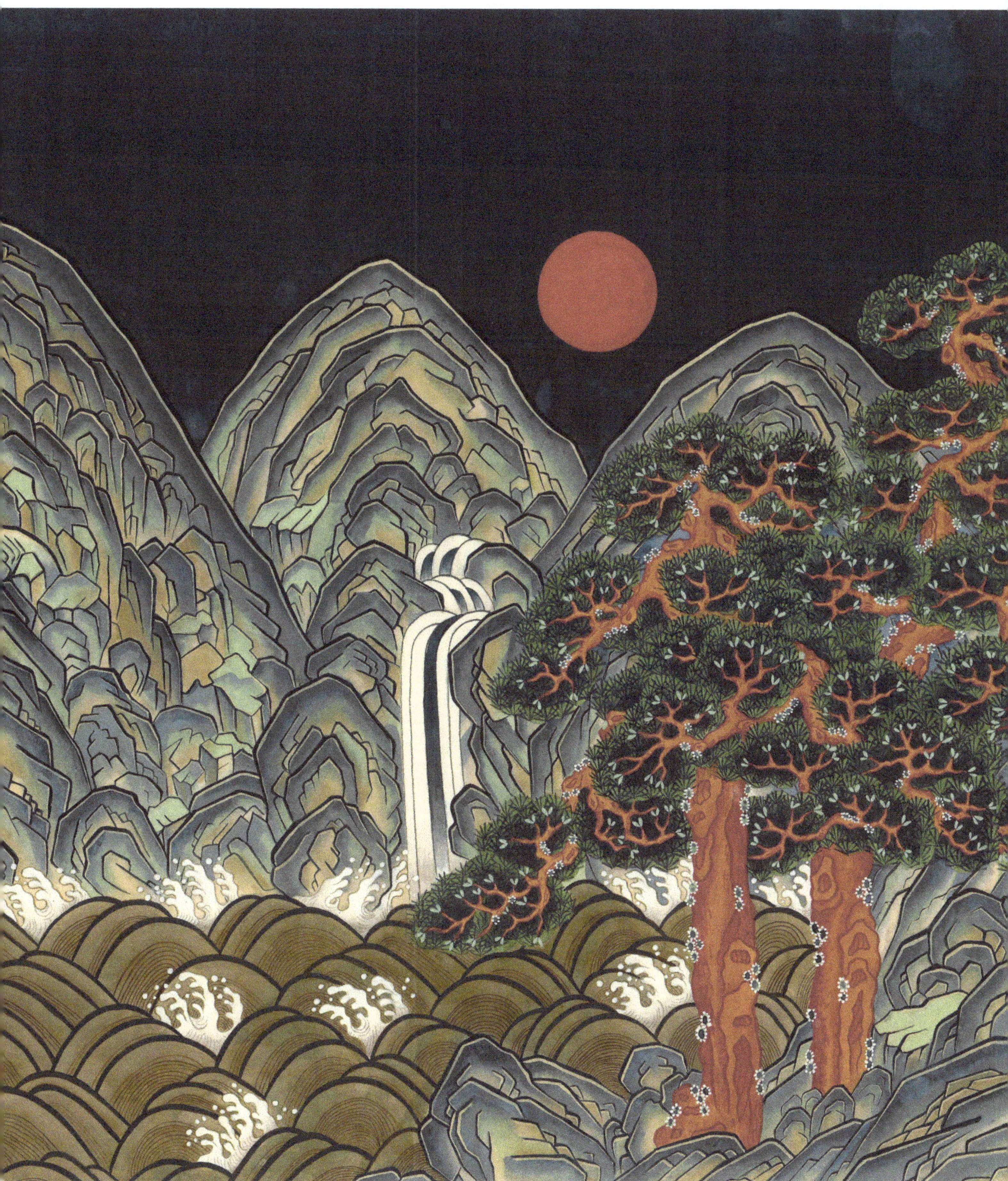

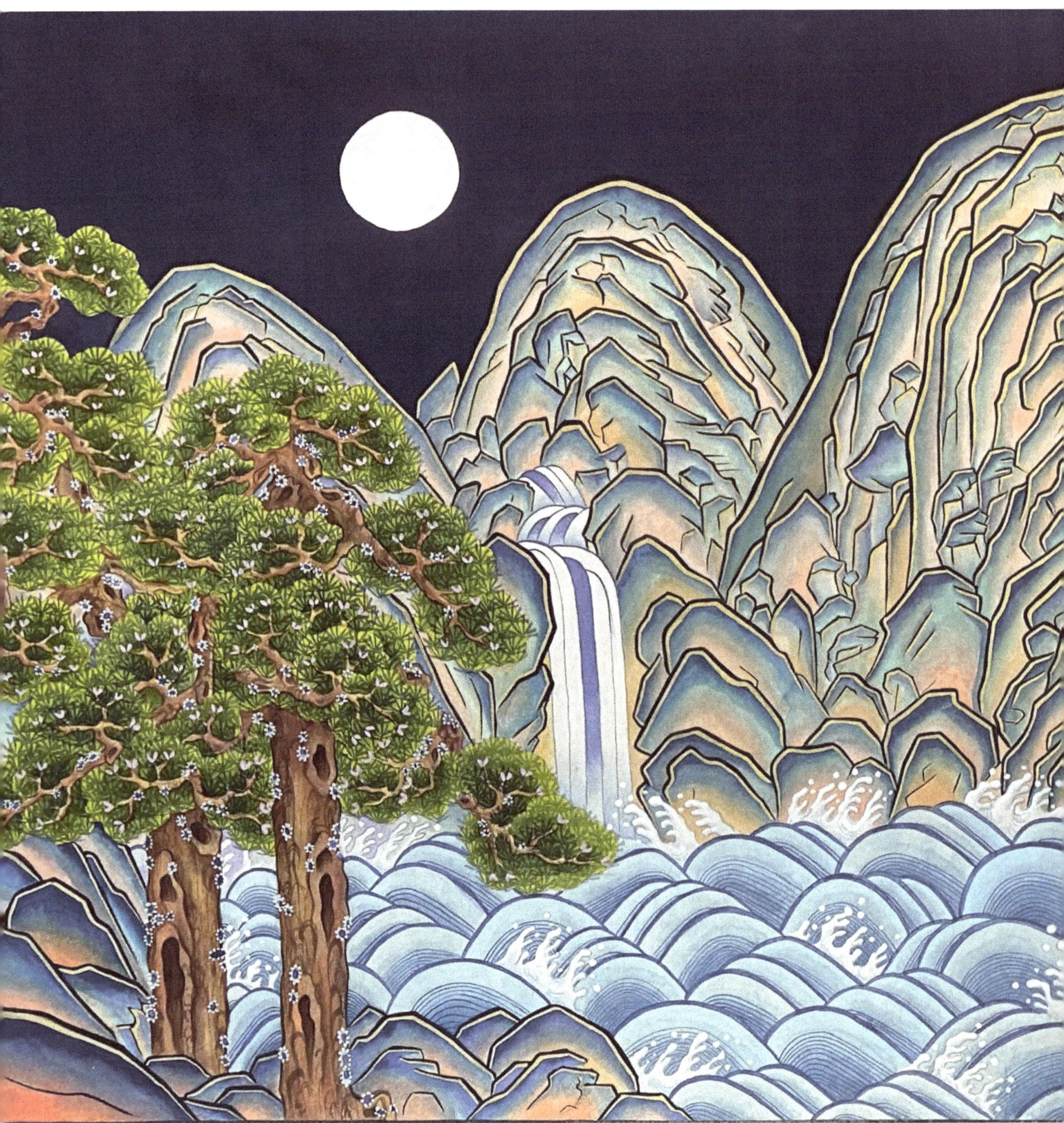

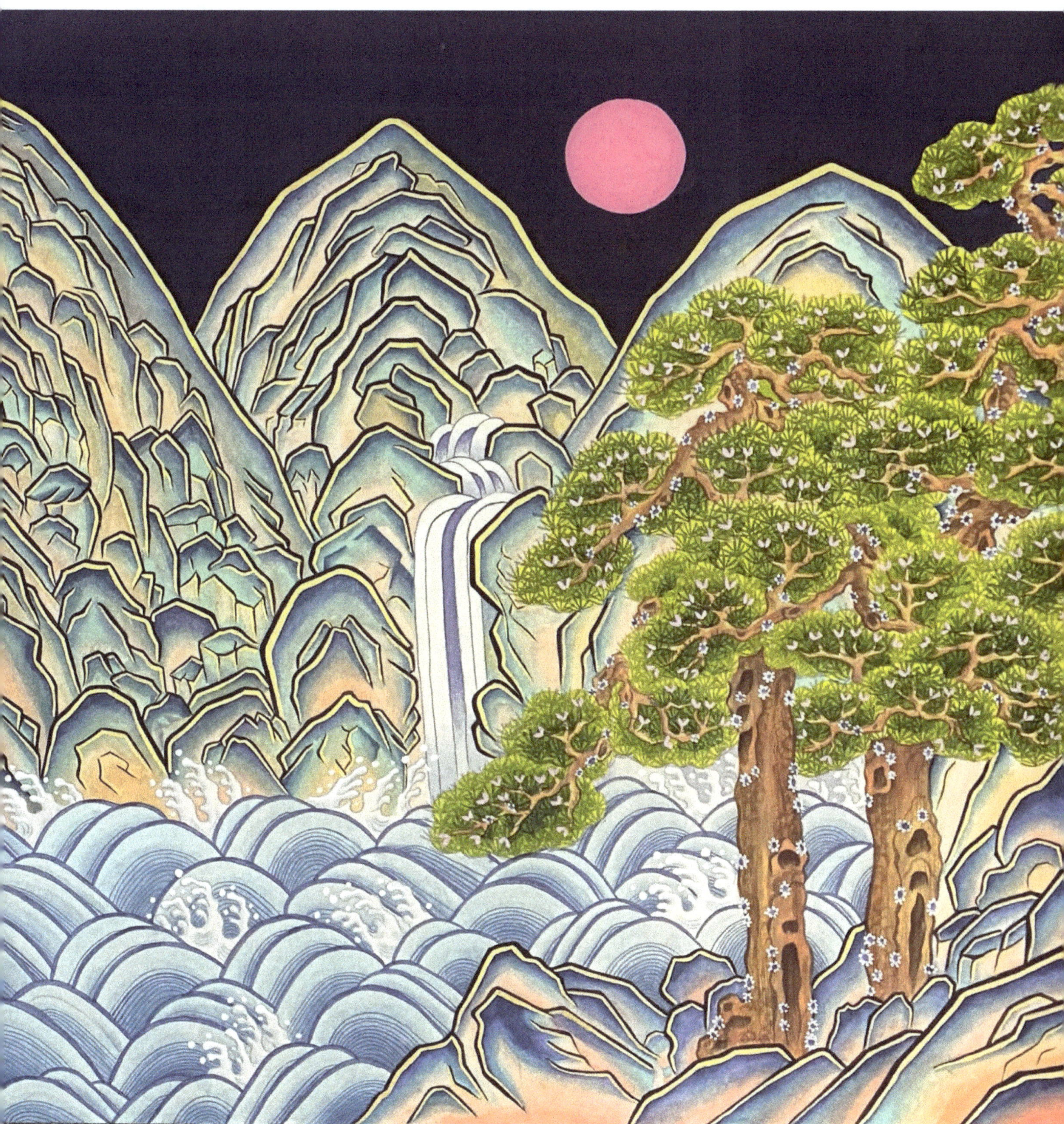

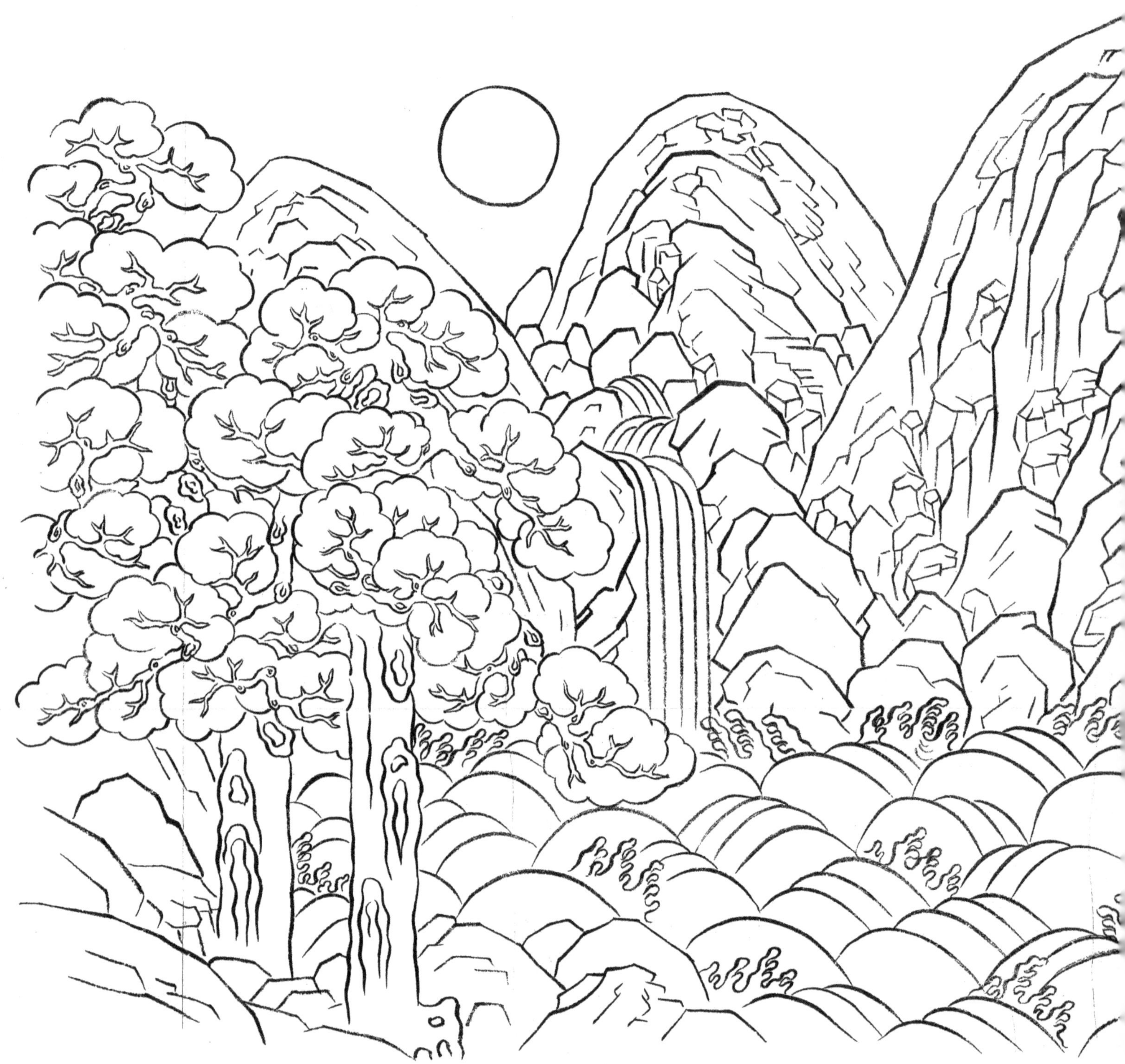

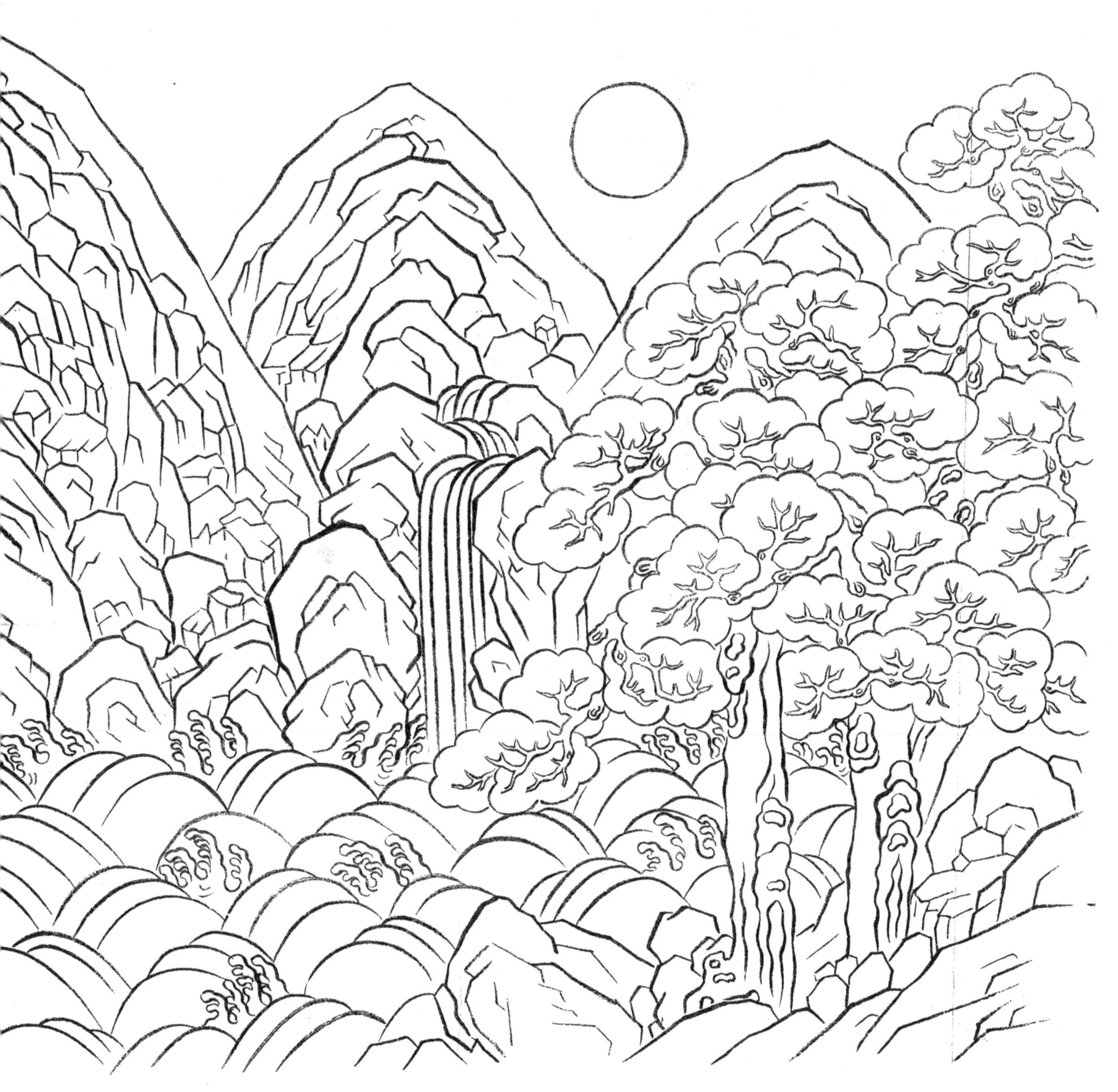

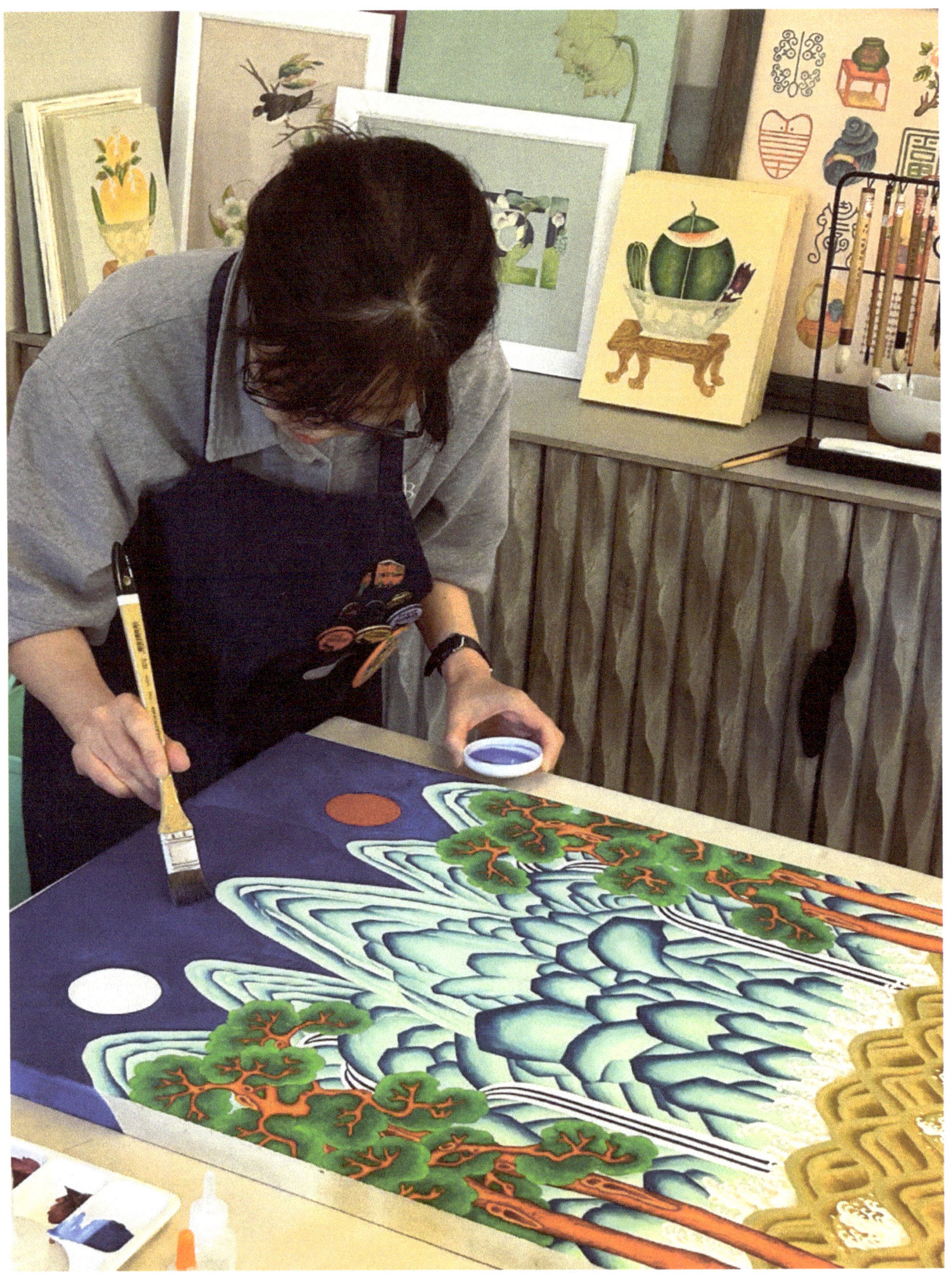

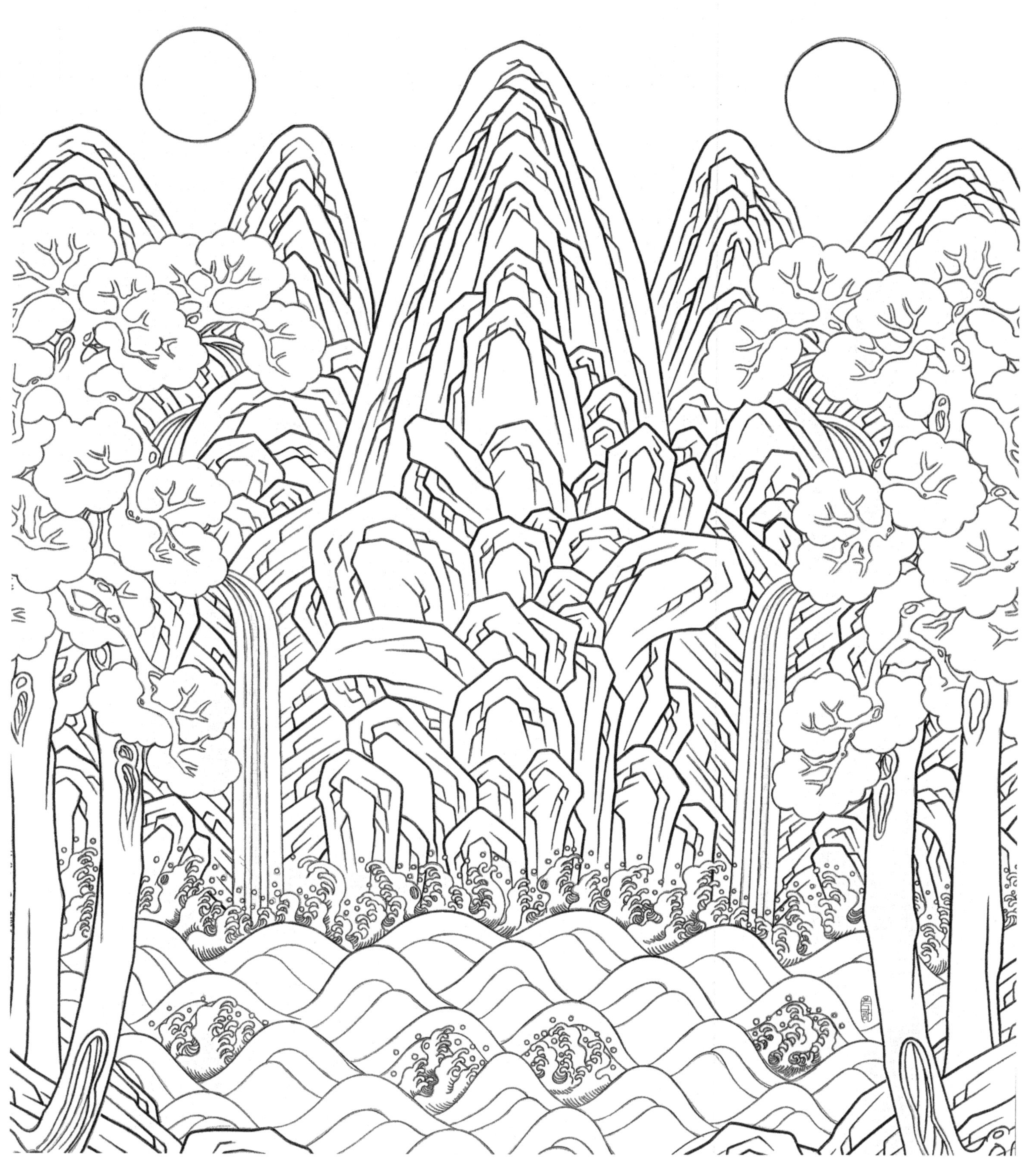

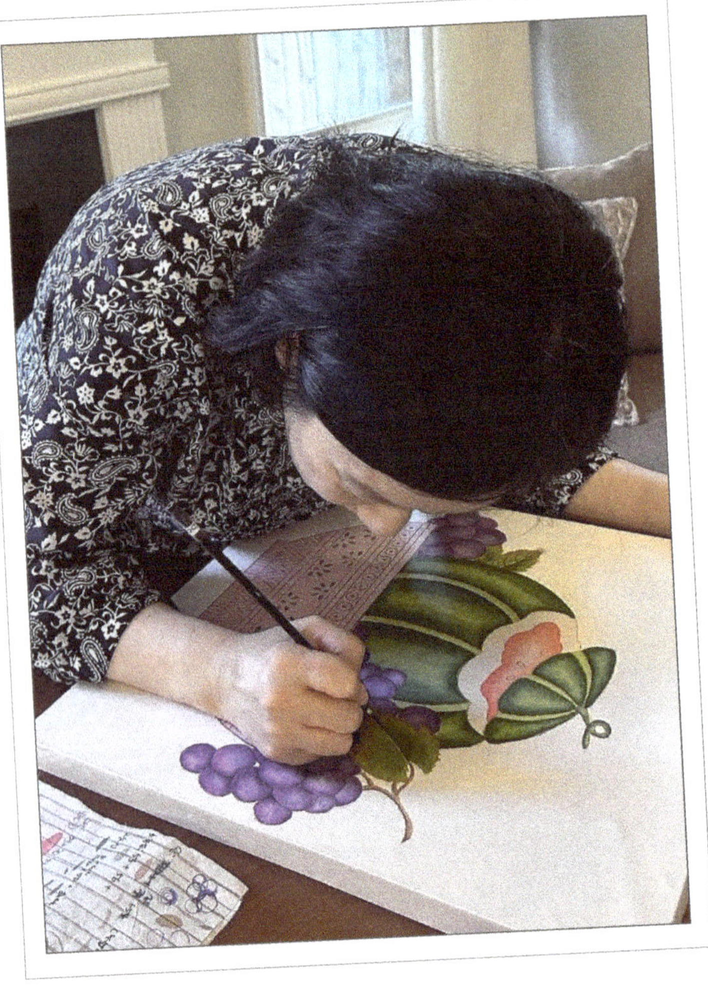
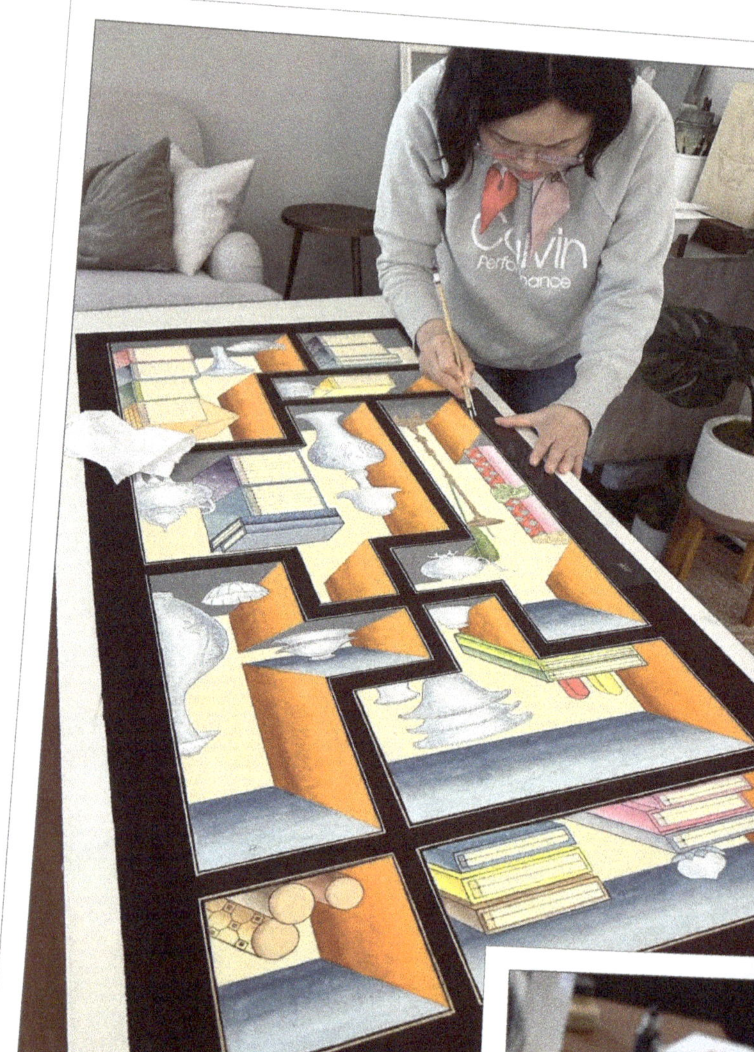
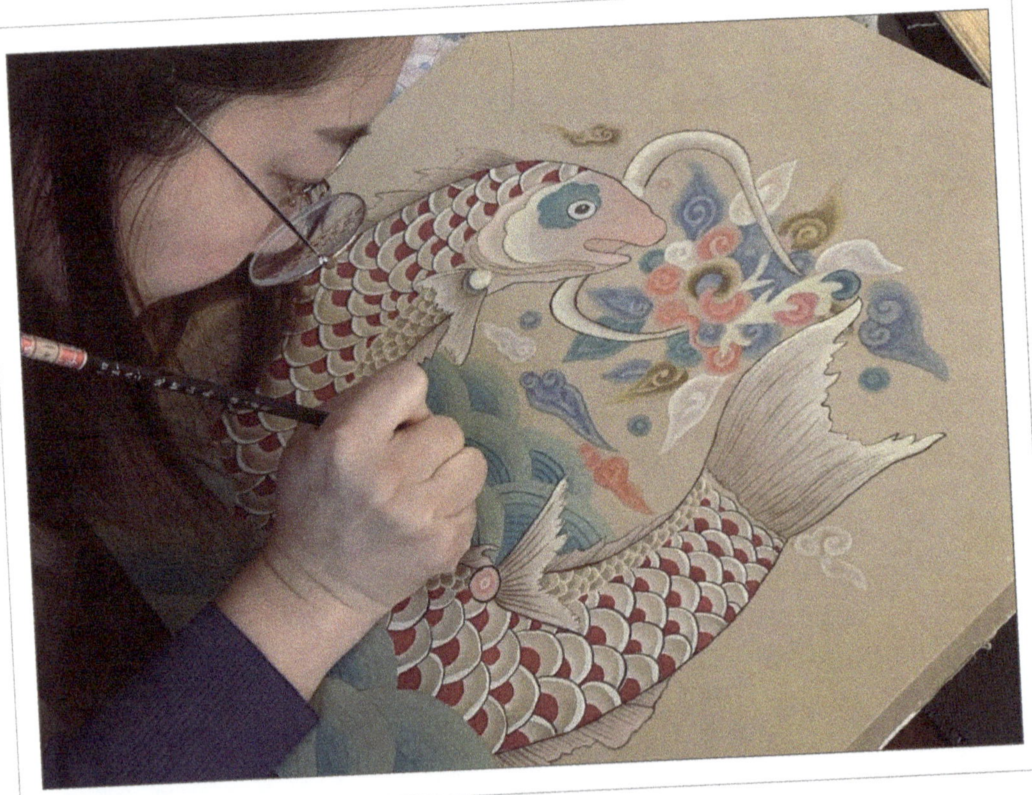

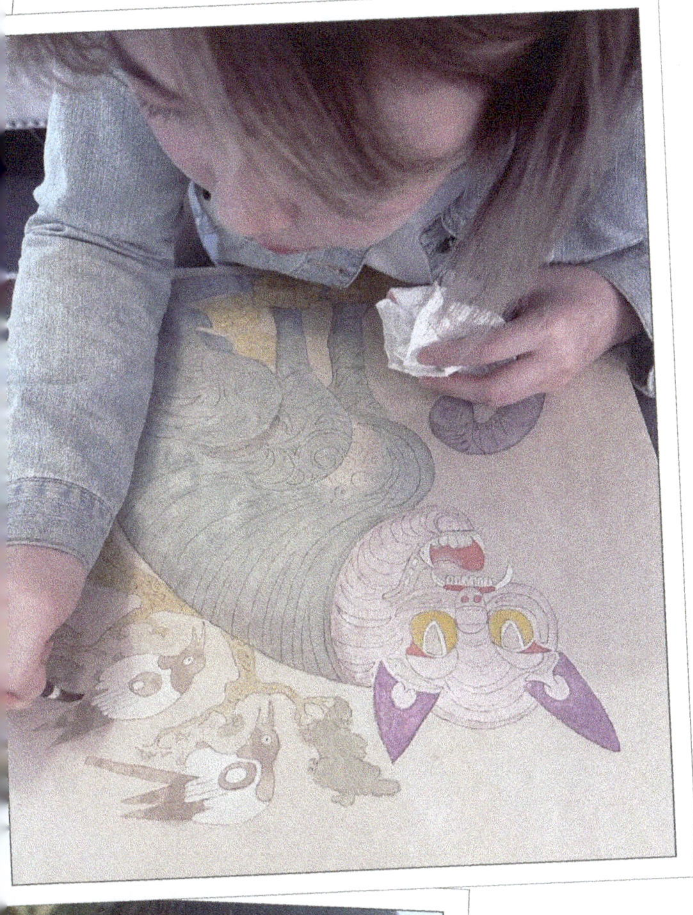
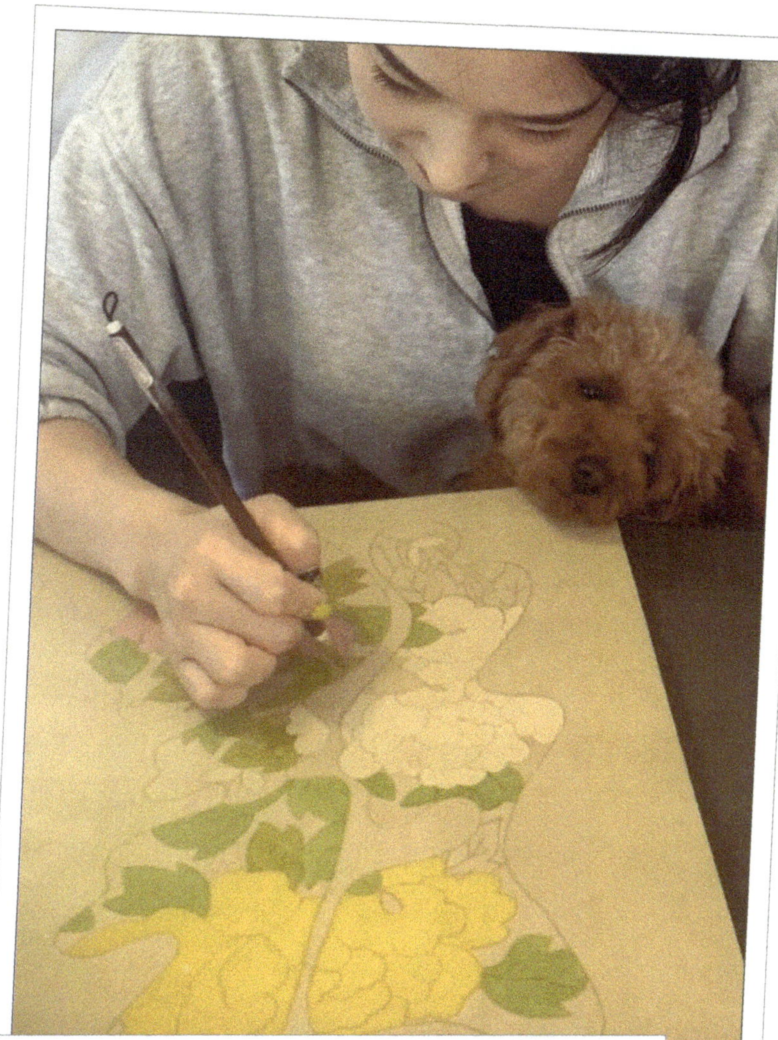
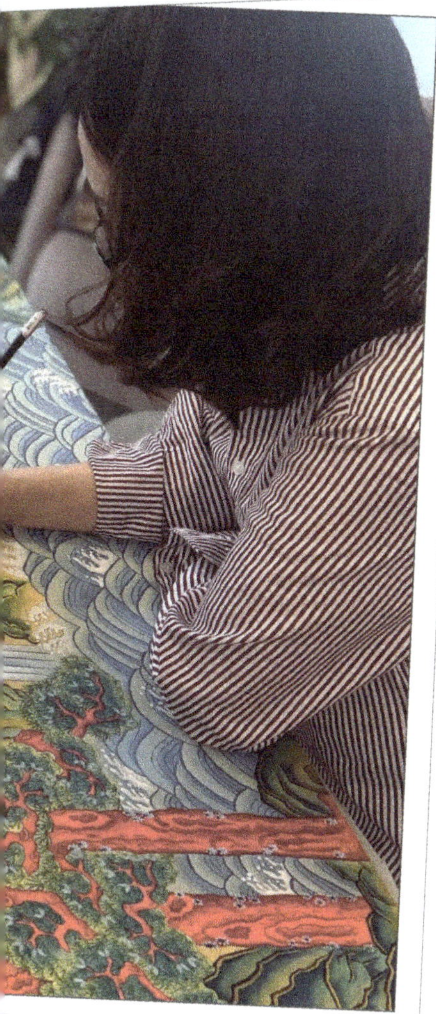
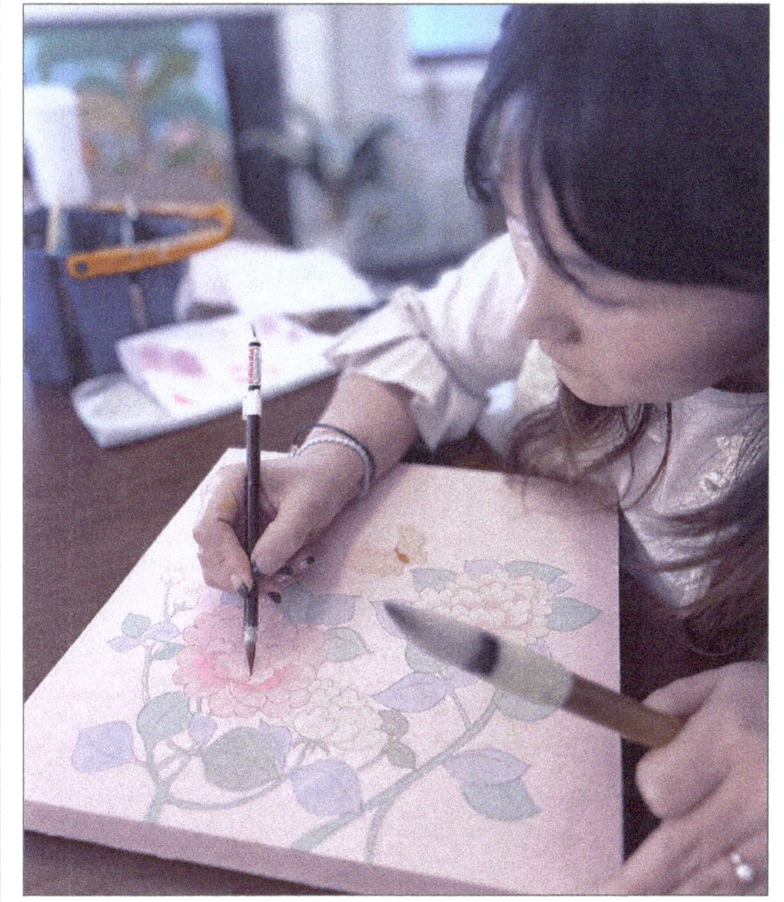

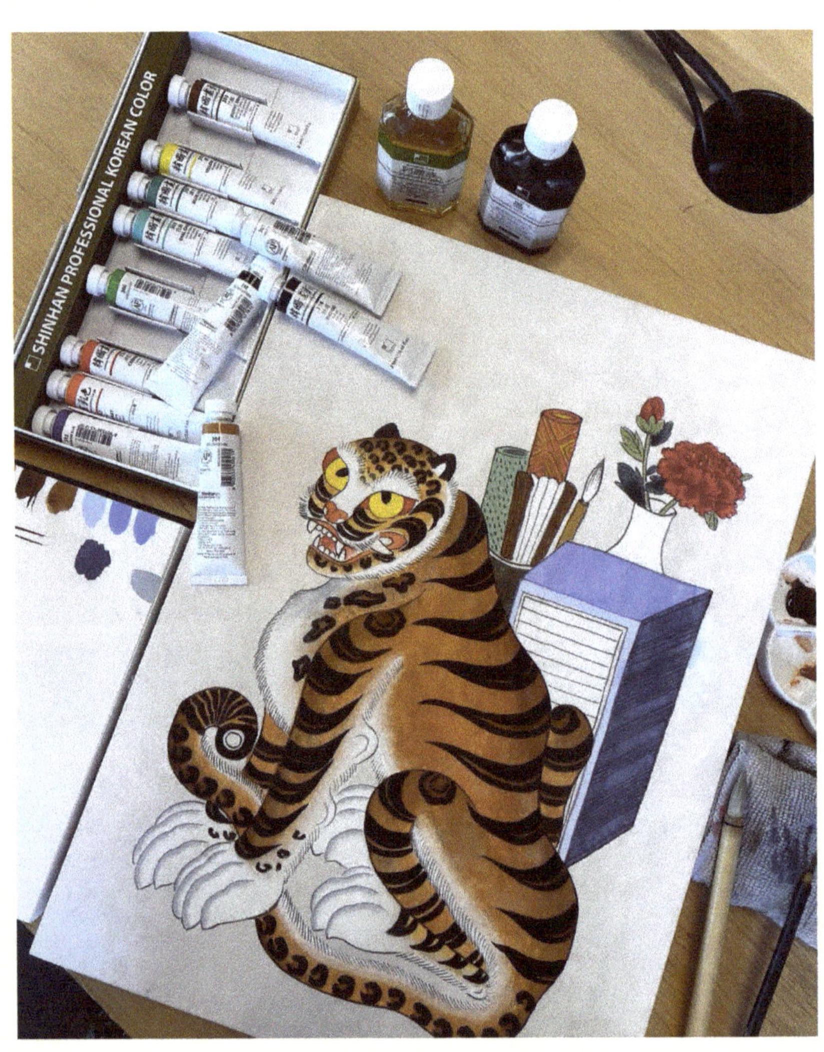

Resources

❁ Resources ❁

Some of the photos included in this book were provided by our partners.
Thank you for your support in spreading the beauty of Korean traditional arts.

Sungsim Pilbang (성심필방)

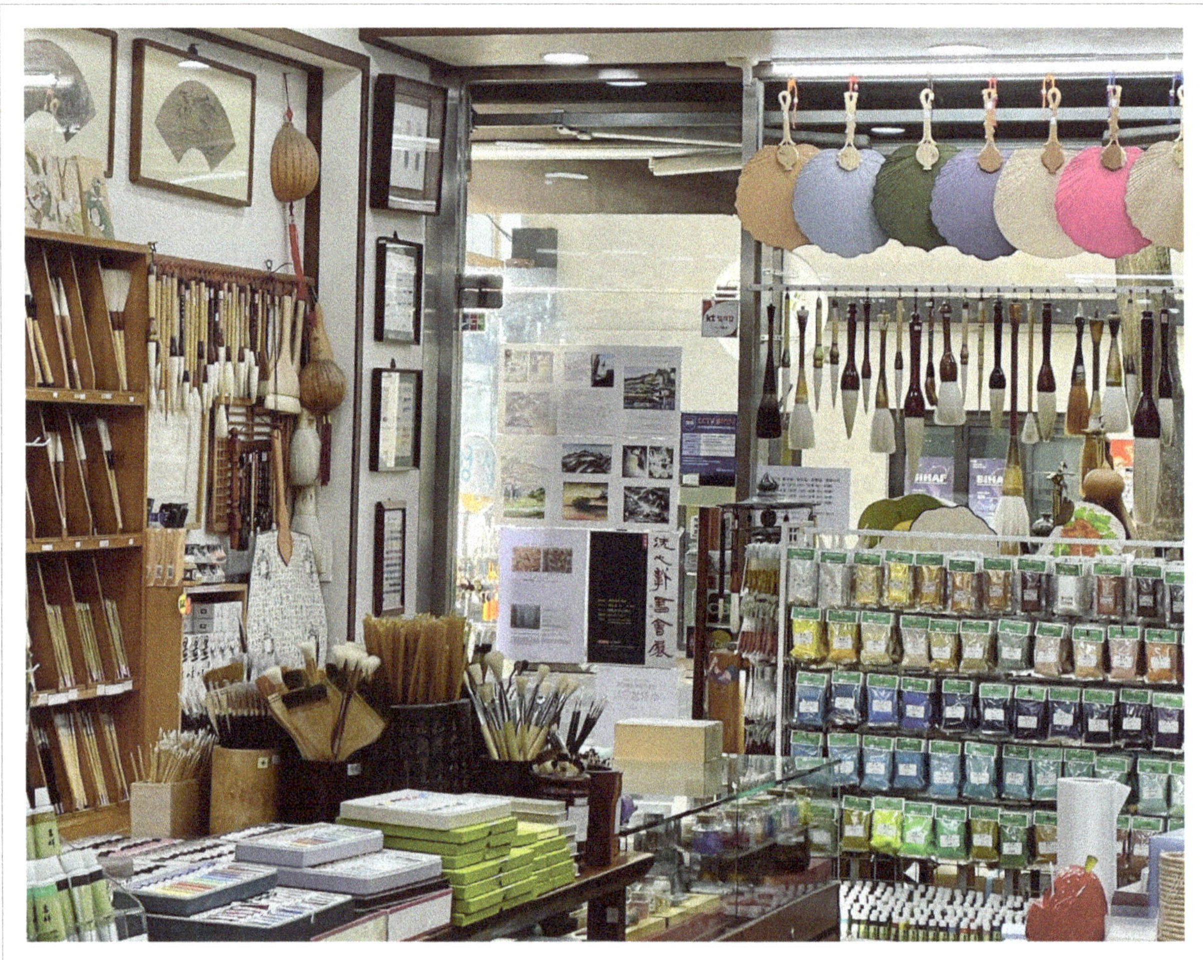

Seoul's premium retailer of Eastern Fine Arts and Calligraphy supplies.
Ships worldwide.

CONTACT +82 10-5123-3313
ADDRESS 14 Insadong-gil, Jongno-gu, Seoul, Republic of Korea
INSTAGRM @sungsimpilbang

ShinHan Art (신한화구)

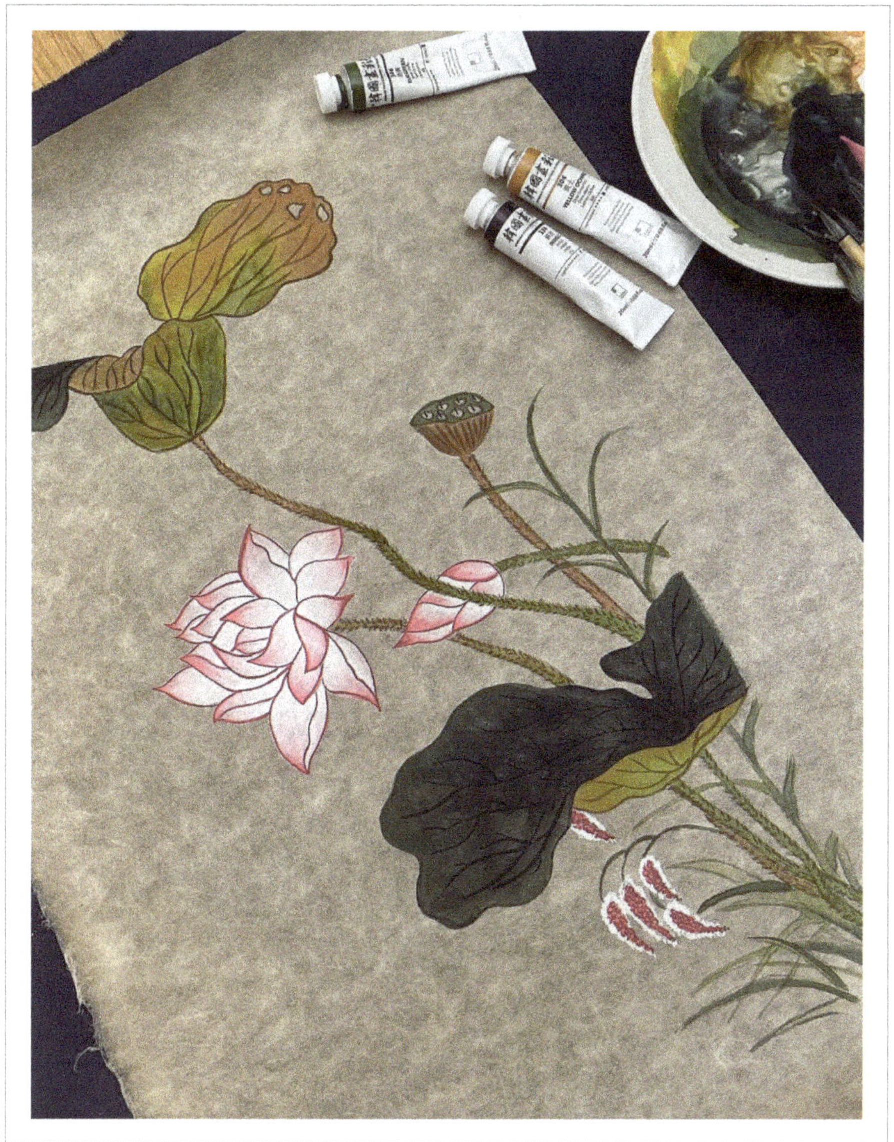

Korea's No.1 Professional Art Materials Company

CONTACT +82-2-357-2651
WEBSITE www.shinhanart.com
EMAIL info@shinhanart.com
INSTAGRM @shinhanart.official / @shinhanart.usa

Alpha Sisters Publishing, LLC
5174 McGinnis Ferry Road #348
Alpharetta, GA 30005
alphasisterspublishing.com

Author: Hye-Ryung Suk
Translator: Seo Choi
Editor: Seo Choi, Sheenah Freitas
Publisher: Seo Choi
Book Designer: Aram Kim

Notes on Images & Illustrations:
The original minhwa artists' names are unknown, unless the artist's name is explicitly stated.
All recoloring of the minhwa arts in this book is by Hye-Ryung Suk and may not be used outside of the book without the publisher's prior written permission.

Library of Congress Cataloging-in-Publication Data is available upon request.

First Edition
ISBN 979-8-9869373-6-6 (paperback)

Printed in the United States of America

www.ingramcontent.com/pod-product-compliance
Lightning Source LLC
Chambersburg PA
CBHW040210110726
48005CB00019B/2969